Dismantling Privilege

Dismantling Privilege

An Ethics of Accountability

Mary Elizabeth Hobgood

The Pilgrim Press

Cleveland, Ohio

For Thomas
and in memory of Eleanor Humes Haney, 1931–1999

The Pilgrim Press, Cleveland, Ohio 44115
© 2000 by Mary Elizabeth Hobgood

Biblical quotations are from the New Revised Standard Version of the
Bible, © 1989 by the Division of Christian Education of the National
Council of Churches of Christ in the U.S.A., and are used by permis-
sion. Adaptations have been made for inclusivity.

Printed in the United States of America on acid-free paper

05 04 03 02 01 00   5 4 3 2 1

Library of Congress Cataloging-in-Publication Data

Hobgood, Mary E., 1946–
    Dismantling privilege : an ethics of accountability / Mary
Elizabeth Hobgood.
        p. cm.
    Includes bibliographical references and index.
    ISBN 0-8298-1374-8 (pbk : alk. paper)
        1. Elite (Social sciences)—United States.   2. Social
stratification—United States.   3. Social ethics.   4. Sociology,
Christian.   I. Title.

HN90.E4 H63 2000
305.5′12′0973—dc21   99-056633

Contents

Preface

This book explores the ethical foundations of contemporary U.S. society by examining systems of routine, systemic, unearned advantage. I uncover the "commonsense" assumptions and institutional power arrangements that accompany the class, race, and gender locations of dominant groups. My goal is to make people like me recognize our unearned privilege and explore our membership in overadvantaged groups. As privileged people seek to honor ethical requirements for accountability, we need to uncover the terms of our participation in multiple sites of unearned advantage.

While this work can never be exhausted in any one study, I build on the work of others as I examine how those with privilege are embedded at the intersection of various power relations that over-advantage us at the expense of subordinate social groups and the environment. It is true that privileged groups are not responsible for systems we did not create. Nevertheless we are accountable to others for the unearned advantages these systems routinely accrue to us, as well as for how we contribute (often unwittingly) to the reproduction of these systems. We are also accountable to ourselves for how these systems distort our human potential and erode justice even for us.

I argue that privileged people are morally damaged, spiritually impoverished, and physically at risk by a society structured to give unfair advantages to the few while it dismisses everyone's needs for respect, affection, just communal relations, and a healthy ecosphere. Drawing upon resources from the Christian tradition, this book seeks to offer the privileged an alternative framework for understanding self and others to the one provided by the liberal ideology of heterosexist, white supremacist, market capitalism. In ethically evaluating social systems with a primary focus on privilege rather than oppression, my goal is to foster Christian solidarity. By unearthing the structural links among diverse systems of privilege and oppression, I hope to foster the formation of alliance politics and a more inclusive democratic practice. This requires that privileged people grow in awareness of what is at stake in the struggle for justice, not only for subordinate groups, but for us as well.

My journey with oppression and privilege began in childhood. Although both of my parents were white, their backgrounds were starkly different. Their interclass marriage during World War II meant that I spent much time in my early years shuttling between two loving grandmothers who lived in completely different worlds—though, as I was later to realize, worlds that were intimately connected. My father's mother was a sharecropper who labored from dawn to dusk in the red clay fields of Mississippi. My mother's mother was a woman of leisure in high-society New Orleans. No matter their economic resources, however, both grandmothers had black women working for them. And to greater or lesser degrees, both experienced disadvantages because my grandfathers were dead.

Although they would not be fully articulated until decades later, fundamental questions were raised for me as I took turns living with these two women and I was repeatedly immersed in such starkly contrasting environments. One month I would be swimming and dining at the country club, and the next picking cucumbers, slopping hogs, and gathering eggs that the undisciplined chickens laid under the house. As a small child, I was concerned and confused about work and poverty, about racial hierarchy and gender subordination, about fairness and justice. These were questions about which the adults around me seemed uninterested or unaware.

I spent my later childhood and adolescence in the relative isolation of suburban America, but these questions reemerged for me in adulthood when I joined a religious community. Working in poor neighborhoods and schools of New York City, while studying the documents of Vatican II and liberation theology, made suffering from exploitation and oppression a daily reality. It also made my privilege, especially as a religious with a vow of poverty, even more apparent.

After I left the convent and married, my ongoing academic work in feminist liberation ethics has helped me see that an exploration of oppression must also be an exploration of privilege. Along with others in my field, I have been encouraged to link my social loca my membership in white, affluent, heterosexual groups. But even more important, feminist liberation ethics must make the connections between the unearned advantages routinely acquired by privileged groups, such as mine, and the unearned disadvantages that are increasing today for persons in groups subordinated by class stratification, white racism, and male dominance.

This work remains pressing to me not only because of my academic commitments but also because of the people in the diverse neighborhoods my family has lived in, and the organizations to which I belong. Living in urban neighborhoods, for example, makes it harder to be oblivious to privilege when some of your neighbors may lack necessities. Such folk have insisted that I become a good ally to them in their struggle for greater justice. Learning how to do this is my ongoing challenge and commitment.

In this process, I work with students who come primarily from elite backgrounds and are preparing themselves to enter the ranks of the privileged as adults. With other teaching colleagues, I struggle not only to help students think more critically about privilege, but also to develop forms of pedagogy that will encourage them to take risks in the community. As students make important connections between themselves and others, they develop moral courage and a political agenda, including accountability to the ecosphere, which may soon be unable to sustain life.

Classroom and field work should help us grow in our understanding of how diverse people are intimately connected through a political economy that uses some groups to benefit others. Linking living and learning in the educational process should help privileged people grow in our understanding not only of how social systems exploit and oppress others as they destroy the ecosphere, but also of how they intensify danger even for elites. As we explore dimensions of mounting peril even for privileged groups, we grow in clarity about what we value, what we oppose, and what we are willing to fight for. We can become more sophisticated in what can be done today to open up small spaces of freedom that will lead to greater emancipation for all social groups and for the environment tomorrow. If we are to take moral responsibility for our lives, we must become aware of the various dimensions of our overprivilege so that we can become accountable for them. I hope that educating elites like myself about our privilege and how it works against justice even for us will make a contribution to this process.

Acknowledgments

Publishing captures a moment in a continuing conversation. Many people helped me with this piece of the conversation. I am grateful to the College of the Holy Cross for a junior leave semester that initiated this book. The Northeast Consultation in Feminist Ethics provided a sounding board in the early stages. To ease the burden of teaching and writing, Jim Nickoloff intercepted and took on work before it reached my door. Jerry Lembcke gave support at a particularly vulnerable time and suggested my working title *Ethics for Elites*. Carolyn Howe is a dialogue partner who always pushes me forward. Alice Laffey and Sara DeMeo helped without knowing it. And deadlines could not have been met without Suzanne Sylvester.

At The Pilgrim Press, I am grateful for Tim Staveteig's kindness and his enthusiasm for this project and for Ed Huddleston's careful attention to details.

I am especially indebted to two Christian ethicists—Elizabeth Bettenhausen and Marvin Ellison—who spent hours reading earlier versions of the manuscript and helped me improve its form and content. As theorists, educators, and activists as well as human beings who are always ready for a good time, they provide enormous inspiration. I am grateful for their friendship, their good company, and all that they have to teach me.

On the home front, I give thanks to the men I live with, the three loves of my life. Nathan dropped encouraging notes and telephoned support from afar. Luke and Tom persevered through a long and grueling time of living in a small apartment with a writer.

Finally, I am grateful to Ellen Marie Keane, R.S.H.M., who first nurtured my critical eye on this world, and to Joan M. Martin for expecting me to do this work.

1

An Ethical Agenda for Elites

How can we come to understand the ethical obligations we have
to one another not only as individuals but as members of
groups?

—Peter J. Haas

On September 3, 1991, the Tuesday after Labor Day, the Imperial
Foods chicken processing plant in Hamlet, North Carolina, caught
fire. Fifty-six of the 200 workers were seriously injured, and 25 workers, primarily women and disproportionately African American, died.
Like the 146 workers of the 1911 New York City Triangle Shirtwaist
Fire, the Imperial Foods workers went to their deaths in a sweatshop-
style industry that disproportionately exploited white women and
people of color. Unlike the Triangle Shirtwaist Fire, however, which
elicited 100,000 people to march down Broadway in a protest that
provoked the unionization of garment workers, the Imperial Foods
fire received little media or political attention.[1]

These stories of workers, disproportionately female and of color,
who suffer and die while the world barely notices are common in our
society and around the world. Such events are juxtaposed against the
reality that the richest 10 percent of shareholders in the United States,
who own 90 percent of outstanding corporate stock, have seen their
dividends increase by more than 250 percent since 1980.[2] These events
are also juxtaposed against the reality of a political economy that, on
the one hand, superexploits and oppresses increasing numbers of
workers at the lowest tiers of the working class and, on the other hand,
offers benefits and unearned advantages primarily to white workers
in the upper tiers of the labor market. The work of this book is to pay
attention to the story of the Imperial Foods disaster and others like it
and to analyze the realities of class exploitation, racism, and sexism
that deeply structure these events. However, more is needed for an

ethic that guides people for living in the real world at the turn of the new century. What is also needed is an ethical framework that connects the growing misery of many to the privilege of a relative few in the society.

My analysis is indebted to Peggy McIntosh, whose seminal essay about "unearned privilege" has helped many of us begin to analyze our membership in groups that grant routine advantages about which we are meant to remain oblivious.[3] We have been socialized to see privilege as a just reward for superior talent and effort and disadvantage as a result of individual inadequacies. Consequently, we are not tutored in uncovering the way society reproduces unshared power arrangements that are often at the root of these privileges and disadvantages. As will be discussed, my analysis assumes that unshared power is at the root of injustice and that uncovering social relations of class, race, and gender that reproduce unshared power and routine unearned advantage for some is the work of ethics.

Although most readers of this book may not be in the richest 10 percent of the population, they are likely to belong to the relatively small percentage of people in our society who, while not necessarily of the upper class, nevertheless enjoy significant unearned advantages because of the privileged groups to which they belong. This study invites all readers to do an ethical analysis of social power and privilege. Those who have relatively more amounts of power and privilege in the class, race, and sex/gender systems are called "elites" in this study. I especially encourage these more privileged readers to make connections between their relatively advantageous social location and the human vocation to create a moral world. I write from an explicitly Christian ethical perspective; however, I trust that my analysis will be helpful to others of differing faiths and of no particular faith tradition.

In the chapters ahead, I address people who are unaware they have unearned benefits through the class, race, and gender systems that impact almost every dimension of our lives. I address people like myself, a white professional woman and practicing heterosexual who, while not among the most powerful in the society, nevertheless routinely receives unearned advantages. We comprise a global minority if we are white and enjoy relative economic affluence. Among us some enjoy other aspects of privileged status in this society that are associated with being able-bodied, heterosexual, or male.

An analysis of group membership reveals that privilege does not come randomly. Having privileged access to the benefits in society is usually not a matter of having good luck or of being fortunate. Neither is privilege solely a matter of personal effort. Routine privilege is largely due to our membership in elite class, race, and gender groups that enjoy unshared power in our society. I will argue that contrary to what most people have been taught, the power of privileged access to social benefits is not distributed primarily through good luck or individual merit. Rather, privilege comes as a result of our dominant positions in interlocking class, race, and sex/gender systems. As we shall see, unearned benefits come when our group has the power to increase the social burden on other groups.

Working Definitions

Differences by way of race, gender, and even class are often considered natural or biologically determined. I follow a different logic: these differences are social in nature.[4] They are constructed in culture and laden with ethical meanings. I will construct class, race, and gender as ways of distinguishing people according to the vested interests of more powerful groups. Class, race, and gender systems construct different identities through unjust power arrangements. These systems are patterns of relations that elites reproduce through their ownership and/or control of the major institutions in the society. Class, race, and gender are not natural or essential attributes of who we are as human beings. Contrary to dominant assumptions, they are not like hair or eye color or blood type. Rather, class, race, and gender distinctions are artificial constructions that mutually condition one another. They have been created historically by the most powerful social groups to serve their interests as these interests change over time. Patricia Hill Collins notes that dominant knowledge assumes that differences lie in the groups themselves rather than in the unjust power relations that construct class, race, and gender difference.[5]

Social constructions of class, race, and gender divide people into groups in order to treat them differently and unfairly in social institutions. These institutions include families, neighborhoods, labor markets, businesses, the medical and legal professions, government, the media, schools, prisons, and the churches. Class, race, and sex/gender relations promoted by these institutions have been carefully constructed by persons with power in the society to routinely give advantages to their groups while increasing the social burdens on others. I will argue that a relative minority in the society use economic, political, and cultural institutions to promote their vested interests at the expense of the majority.

Powerful groups are called "elites" or "the privileged" or "dominants" in this study. For our purposes here, the most powerful group in the society includes those with the greatest advantages in all three systems. They belong to the capitalist class and are overwhelmingly white and male. As previously mentioned, they are located in the upper 10 percent of the population who, in 1995, owned and controlled more than 70 percent of the wealth, including 90 percent of the value of all stock.[6] Most of this group's income is made not from wages and salaries but from income-producing properties. This group makes the major decisions that drive the economy, the political process, and major cultural institutions. The power of this group includes the ability to define the economic interests, cultural values, and patterns of social behavior that are imposed on everyone.[7] This group enjoys most of the benefits in the society and creates unjust burdens for the majority.

Immediately below it, however, are the groups to whom this study is addressed: elites who enjoy some of the class, race, and gender benefits of the most privileged. As we shall see, we enjoy unearned benefits to the degree that we are essential to the work of reproducing the class, race, and sex/gender systems. We enjoy relative social power even though we may also occupy subordinate social locations. For example, we may be white and also gay, economically affluent and also female, white heterosexual male and also disabled. We must therefore acquire a sense of our relative power within a variety of dominant/subordinate relations.

For purposes of my argument, the elites addressed here enjoy more dominance than we suffer subordination. We are disproportionately white, heterosexual, and male. We are not members of the capitalist class, but like them, we derive unearned benefits and advantages from the lower tiers of the working class. We are professionals and managers in the upper tiers of the working class, or those preparing to enter those tiers. Most of us are not, at least yet, subjected to a significant erosion of our relative control over work or the disappearance of our jobs, which has been endemic to the lower tiers of the working class. We gain status by separating ourselves from other workers and calling ourselves "middle class." We separate out as middle class even though, like all workers, we have only or primarily our productive abilities to sell for a wage in order to sustain ourselves and our families. At the same time we do not acknowledge that our income, compared to most wage earners, is anything but middle. We include those whose incomes have been steady or rising, whose households in 1997 earned as much as $80,000 or more and thought of ourselves as middle class even though almost 80 percent of U.S. households earned less than we did.[8]

It is my purpose to show ways in which those in privileged groups, ourselves included, use institutions to socialize people into "proper" dominant and subordinate class, race, and sex/gender identities and roles. These proper identities and roles shape what people think and value, how they act, and the degree to which they feel entitled to the benefits of society or blame themselves for disproportionately bearing its burdens. Such identities enable elites to enjoy, to greater or lesser degrees, selective access to the material and symbolic benefits in the society. Most damaging of all, these socially constructed identities oblige most people in the society to act against their long-term interests so that elites can receive short-term benefits.[9]

This situation is constantly reproduced when unequal power relations are hidden within "commonsense" assumptions that mystify our class, race, and gender locations.[10] Our society has successfully normalized the social relations that comprise class, race, and gender systems and the unshared power arrangements they reproduce. As a consequence, poor female workers of color routinely suffer and die in sweatshops, and such events get buried in the back pages of newspapers. We experience the social relations that mediate class exploitation and gender and race oppression as normal and natural. We do not notice how the patterned behaviors we engage in daily, either as individuals or as affiliates of institutions, exploit, silence, disable, or marginalize some as they confer status, profits, and other benefits on elites.

My task in this book is to analyze the class, race, and sex/gender systems and to challenge our customary assumptions about them. I will argue that the identities and roles reproduced at various institutional sites, such as families, labor markets, and the media, often reinforce one another and maintain a class-stratified, white supremacist, heterosexist, and male-dominant society. Analysis of institutional sites of human interaction that mediate class, race, and gender power is for a distinctive purpose: to encourage alternative ways of acting and the creation of new social systems where power is more equitably shared.

Groups that are disadvantaged by the class, race, and sex/gender systems, called "subordinates" in this study, are usually aware, at least to some degree, of how institutions work to disempower them and how they carry a disproportionate share of the burdens in the society. It also remains true that, although power may be disproportionately waged by a few groups, elites never monopolize it totally. While they wield massive institutional and ideological control of subordinates, as our investigation will uncover, the most privileged groups also depend on the cooperation of subordinates, including those like ourselves who enjoy some dimensions of elite status, to maintain the status quo. Since every dependency is in reality an interdependency, the better we understand the way class, race, and sex/gender systems work, the more we see where dominants are vulnerable and where subordinates have at least some power under some conditions.[11] Some subordinates are aware of this and exercise their power to resist their subordination. As we shall see, the work of solidarity is extremely important, since the costs to subordinates when they claim their own power are inversely proportionate to the numbers who engage in resistance.

My focus in this book, however, is not on subordinate groups but on those who enjoy relatively more amounts of social privilege than they suffer subordination. As I have noted, most people in privileged groups have little notion that systems mediating disproportionate advantage to them even exist. Since class, race, and sex/gender systems make unearned advantages for dominants and unearned disadvantages for subordinates seem normal and natural, they are "commonsense" to elites.

Thus, I am not concerned with what dominants *intend*, for many people privileged to greater or lesser degrees by class, race, and gender have only good intentions and wish harm to no one. Rather, I am concerned with what privileged groups *effect* through their ownership, control, and reproduction of the major institutions in the society.[12] I wish to address people like myself, who occupy dominant positions in at least some of the three systems examined here. How various institutions reproduce our class, race, and/or sex/gender privilege becomes visible to us only when we work to analyze them. Demonstrating the connection between unearned privilege and unearned disadvantage is essential if we are to understand more realistically our responsibilities as Christian moral agents.

Why the Privileged Should Dismantle Privilege

As a Christian ethicist, I am concerned with the institutional dynamics that reproduce systems of privilege for the few not only because these systems are unjust for subordinate groups but also because they promote cultural values and social relations that damage everyone. Class, race, and sex/gender systems enable those values to achieve normative status in the society that serve only the vested interests of the few *while they limit everyone's choices and impoverish the quality of all relationships.* Such "values" include the work ethic of discipline, overwork, and managerial control over increasing sectors of labor. They include the sex/gender pseudovalues of entitlement for men and self-sacrifice for women, and a highly regulated marriage ethic for everyone. These values also include an ethic for white normative status that reinforces dominant class and sex/gender values by requiring obsessiveness about work and restrictions on mutual emotional and sexual expression even for elites.

Obsessiveness about work, managerial control over work, and restrictions on friendship, intimacy, and community violate nonnegotiable aspects of human beings that I believe social systems must honor.

discussed below, these aspects or characteristics are grounded in ir fundamentally communal nature. They include the need for self-awareness, affection, respect, sexual fulfillment, and self-management over one's activities, especially one's work.[13] When social systems reproduce ignorance about the connections between self and others, when they isolate people from one another and destroy community, when they stigmatize erotic desire and restrict friendship and intimacy, and when they intensify managerial control over work, they are harmful to everyone. This applies also to elites even when such systems bring unearned advantages to them.

In addition, the class, race, and sex/gender systems, as well as the values that sustain them, are dimensions of ecological domination that jeopardize everyone's survival and well-being. As class, race, and gender are social constructions made by the powerful to condone the unjust treatment of "inferior" categories of human beings, so the non-human world is identified with inferior groups and is subject to injustice. The relations of elites to less-powerful human groups are also reflected in their relations to the biosphere, which is plundered, exploited, raped, and regulated like those in subordinate classes, races, and genders.

Consequently, while we might be tempted to think that only those routinely disadvantaged by class, race, and sex/gender structures would wish to change them, *I argue that everyone should want to change them because these systems, and the values and social relations they promote, harm even the privileged.* We need to investigate not only how class, race, and the sex/gender systems confer undeserved privilege on elites, but also how they confer pseudovalues, impoverished social relations, limited consciousness, and ecological destruction that diminish elites. Therefore, a Christian ethic worthy of the name must investigate how dominant behavior patterns and cultural values deeply distort and impoverish all relationships, even those of the privileged. Political theorist Michael Parenti says, "The power of the system operates even over those who are its more powerful participants."[14] The system imposes its necessities even over the needs of individual elites.

Yet privileged groups are largely uninterested in analyzing these structures, perhaps because they mistakenly believe they have only their privileges to lose. When elites analyze systems, as in liberal political theory or neoclassical economic theory, their point of view typically justifies the status quo. Because I am interested in showing how elites are also damaged, I wish to analyze social systems from a critical rather than a self-justifying point of view. Therefore, I am grateful to the analyses developed by subordinate groups and their allies whose perspective is informed by an alternative consciousness. They do not benefit from class, race, and gender dominance, but must bear unjust social burdens as a result of them.

Privileged people need to become familiar with critical social analysis because it increases self-awareness and offers a moral assessment of social relations. People are like soft putty, shaped by the repeated impact of persons, events, systems, and institutions. Critical social analysis helps us discern how we are constructed as persons through patterned and very ordinary relations of domination and subordination. We can gain some control over the persons we wish to become only if we use social analysis to make a moral evaluation of how unshared power is continually misshaping us and our relations with others. Understanding the workings of class, race, and sex/gender systems is basic to an ethical life because these systems, and the institutional interactions that reproduce them, deeply condition the morality of our lives-in-relation.

In sum, ethical analysis should help us in the project of discerning unjust power arrangements in our relationships with persons, creatures, and the planet itself. This is a first step in a longer process of struggle to change these arrangements. Analysis should also help us understand how unshared power damages us all, including the moral damage suffered by those who seek to monopolize power. Even though groups are harmed in significantly different ways, everyone is profoundly damaged by these fundamental social systems that limit our choices, treat people unfairly, destroy community, and impoverish most aspects of our lives. In addition, we need to discern how class, race, and gender interactions condition us to accept the massive exploitation and destruction of the earth and the environment. *Basic cultural literacy, including our self-understanding as socially constructed persons and our ability to morally evaluate social relations, is at stake in this work, for elites as well as nonelites.*

The Moral Ambiguity of Being Elite

Systems of privilege and the values they promote damage the privileged themselves, so much so that elites suffer a moral pathology. At the same time, the moral responsibility of most elites is complex and ambiguous. For one reason, most elites occupy locations of dominance and subordination simultaneously. Insofar as we belong to one or more subordinate groups in the class, race, and sex/gender systems, we may be tempted to deny our role as dominants in reproducing economic exploitation and political and cultural oppression for others. For example, we may have compassion for people of color, white women, or gays and lesbians, but lack awareness of our participation in exploitation, oppression, and self-righteousness as affluent people, whites, or males.

Insofar as we occupy multiple social locations, the lack of power and freedom we experience from our membership in subordinate groups may blind us to the power we have as members of dominant groups. Our moral situation is complex. We must acknowledge both our pain and our privilege, both how we are constrained and where we have power, if we are to attain responsible moral agency.

Our moral responsibility as elites is further complicated by our relatively sheltered lives. In order to maintain benefits not accessible to others, we value innocence in the forms of ignorance, arrogance, and isolation. We live largely within class- and race-segregated environments in which it is easy to assume that the advantages and resources at our disposal are accessible to others. Ignorance, arrogance, and isolation protect our unearned benefits while keeping us in conformity to the status quo.

However, ignorance, arrogance, and isolation as ways of being in the world also violate the fundamental characteristic of who we are as human beings—selves-in-relation. The ambiguous dimensions of our moral situation become apparent as we become aware of how the roles we play and the values we live by are shaped by systems that, because they isolate us, deeply impoverish the quality of our social relations with people, earth creatures, and the ecosphere.

As the political economy polarizes society even further, privileged groups are experiencing erosion in privileges and status. The moral ambiguity of our situation is revealed when we see that some of this erosion includes loss not only of unfair advantage but also of entitlements, such as decent work, nutritious food, and adequate health care that a just society should make available to all. In addition, when our whiteness or maleness no longer protects us from the harshest fallout of the status quo, and we do not understand the dynamics of our social system, we are ready to believe that conventional scapegoats are the cause of our problems. Fiercely waged by the religious and political Right, scapegoating has intensified in recent decades as it becomes even more necessary to divide dominant groups from the subordinated groups whose ranks we may soon be joining.

Investigating moral pathology and the ambiguity of our moral situation is a difficult task because what most of us know about ourselves and the world has been largely shaped by people who have vested interests in preserving the status quo. Such knowledge is developed by people in the privileged class, race, and gender groups who have power in the institutions that shape cultural practice. Italian Marxist Antonio Gramsci defined "hegemonic knowledge" as knowledge developed by dominant groups in the society to further their own monopolization of power.[15] It is often the only knowledge available to people because it supports conformity to the status quo. This knowledge is transmitted through families, schools, churches, businesses, the media, government, and the medical and legal professions. Dominant groups with power in these institutions create discourses, including the myths, symbols, language patterns, and knowledge through which we understand ourselves as "properly"—that is, hierarchically—classed, raced, and gendered persons. They also shape cultural practice, such as the work ethic and sexual behavior, further regulating fundamental aspects of our lives.

The most powerful are also deeply conditioned by these values and institutions that rarely reveal how power is inequitably shared in the society. Powerful groups shape institutions and cultural values, which in turn shape and misshape them. Consequently, people remain ignorant about precisely how some groups have privileged access to resources at the expense of others. People are also ignorant about how most people, even members of privileged groups, are in danger of losing resources that a just society would make available to all.

People who spend long years exposed to dominant knowledge, values, and behavior patterns believe that the status quo represents the natural order of things. The elites I address here are intensely indoctrinated into the logic of the system since such education provides the resources that elites need for the task of reproducing the society. Another dimension of the complexity of our moral agency is that we often lose power when we challenge unjust systems. Elites maintain their privilege only insofar as they conform to the status quo and make significant contributions to promote it.

What we learn to think about ourselves and others is limited by our unique circumstances of personal biography, by our social location, including our dominant positions in some or most of the class, race, and sex/gender groups, and by our intense exposure to the knowledge created by those who are most powerful in these groups. We are largely unaware that the framework of meaning that informs our consciousness as moral agents has been created by those whose concern is not to enlighten us about how unshared power permeates and impoverishes social relations. As a consequence, many of us suffer ignorance about the way the world is experienced by people in the subordinate positions of the class, race, and gender systems. Their knowledge of the social world is not easily available to us.

Those who seek to monopolize power in class, race, and gender interactions are the minority in the U.S. population. Those who exercise relatively less power in homes, neighborhoods, labor markets, businesses, schools, government, the media, the medical and legal professions, and the churches are the majority. They include working-class/working-poor people; many white women; people of color; gay, lesbian, bisexual, and transgendered people; people with disabilities; children; other creatures; and the ecosystem itself. These groups, which overlap at many points, do not hear or read much that describes the world from their point of view. The perspectives of the economically exploited, politically oppressed, and culturally marginalized majority are certainly largely unknown to the minority in dominant positions.

The ambiguity of our moral agency as privileged people who have little access to subordinate knowledge and suffer relative social isolation is illustrated by an article in my local newspaper. A front page story tells of the release of a Canadian drilling company owner after ninety-four days of captivity in Latin America. Norbert Reinhart was held hostage by a Colombian revolutionary group struggling for peasant agrarian reform. Reinhart was owner and chief executive of a company that was subcontracted by a Canadian mining company to search for gold in the Angostura region of Colombia. Reinhart gave himself as a substitute hostage for an employee who had been captured by the Revolutionary Armed Forces of Colombia. Reinhart, justly hailed as a hero who risked his life for another, made little of his efforts and pointed to the suffering of his family and friends who agonized about his survival and well-being. He said his captivity was simply a moral response to the situation of his employee.[16]

I think most people would agree that Norbert Reinhart is a human being who manifests exemplary courage and compassion. We deeply admire his compassion for his employee and his willingness to do what he believed was just and right, even at enormous personal risk. We also need to notice that although Reinhart was attuned to the well-being of an employee in an extraordinary way, he seemed little attuned to his captors. They were the men, women, and children who were dispossessed of the land upon which his company was mining. He described them as decent folk who allowed him to subsist on rice and beans.

Reinhart feels responsibility to his employee but not to thousands of hungry and homeless families whose ancestors once farmed land now confiscated by foreign businesses. As a drilling company owner, he also does not have critical consciousness of how mining dangerously impacts the ecosphere. Without critical social analysis Reinhart lacks awareness of the relationship between the suffering of human and nonhuman nature and the lucrative profits made by his company. Without analysis of class and race, without knowledge of how these systems are embedded in the historical processes of colonialism, neocolonialism, current neoliberal economic policy, and ecological destruction, justice-oriented people like Norbert Reinhart are not tuned in to or responsive to injustices.

It is easy for people in dominant positions to remain ignorant about how systems work to advantage a privileged few and deeply disadvantage the majority. This ignorance directly feeds arrogance when we assume that the world works for others the way it works for us. People with an arrogant sense of entitlement, built on ignorance of how their entitlement comes at the expense of others, suffer a moral pathology in need of relief and repair.

Elites living in ignorance, arrogance, and relative isolation from other groups are also deprived of friendship and community with people, other creatures, and the earth. Reinhart's relatively superficial encounter with the men, women, and children who were his captors shows the normalcy of using others for our purposes or dismissing them as irrelevant to our lives. Knowledge created by dominant groups and promulgated by such institutions as schools, churches, government, and the media anesthetizes our minds and hearts by keeping us from interrogating the structures that mediate our privilege and understanding how privilege is connected to other people's suffering. We become further isolated when others see us as moral pygmies because, in order to deny preferential treatment, *we resist fundamental questions of politics and ethics.*

Avoidance of responsible moral agency is easy for elites who occupy ambiguous locations of both privilege and subordination, live relatively isolated lives that support ignorance and arrogance, are overexposed to education that naturalizes the status quo, and risk losing privileges when we challenge business as usual. That is the bad news. The good news is that our potential for moral agency is enhanced when we explore how systems of privilege hurt others and distort the minds and hearts of the privileged. What is adversely affected is not only our knowledge of the world, but also our fundamental humanity as communal beings created to live in interdependence with others and in accountability to them.

Social Theory and Christian Ethics

Christian vocation has fundamentally to do with making justice in the world. *However, to act justly in the world, we need to know how the world works.* We need a better grasp of the interlocking structure of class, race, and sex/gender systems. We need to know how these systems mediate social interactions. Only then can we evaluate them in light of Christian principles of justice and solidarity. Only then will

we be in a position to form alliances with others and address unsh
power arrangements and social injustice.

Christian ethicist Beverly Harrison writes that all theological ethics have to do with questions of power.[17] Power is good when democratically shared in the service of the commonweal. Democratically
shared power promotes critical self-awareness, self-management, and
responsible interdependence. Democratically shared power promotes
justice and the flourishing of the whole creation. Power is unjust when
elite groups define economic interests, cultural values, and patterns
of social behavior that are imposed on others to the benefit of elites
and the destruction of the natural world.

Ethics has to do with the moral evaluation of social relations as
they are mediated in and through systems that reproduce unshared
power. Ethics needs critical social theory that challenges rather than
justifies present arrangements. Critical social theory "names and maps
out the general organization of social relations" so that people can
better understand their relationship to unshared economic, cultural,
and political power.[18]

Critical social theory helps us explain the systems that structure
our personal and collective experience. It helps us analyze class, race,
gender, sexuality, and ecological dynamics that mediate unshared
power and define our social reality. These systems, often invisible to
those who benefit from them, put powerful constraints on the majority of people in this society who are socially constructed as subordinates and restricted in their ability to live dignified human lives. These
systems are intimately interconnected and mutually shape and reshape
one another. They are interlocking and they reinforce one another
even as they sometimes work in contradiction. As the following chapters will make evident, it is difficult to analyze one without looking at
the others. The class, race, and sex/gender systems are so essential for
one another's reproduction that it is almost impossible to argue which
is more fundamental.

Some social theories, such as liberal political theory and neoclassical economic theory, support these systems. They "innocently" maintain that current economic, political, and cultural arrangements are
inevitable. Other theories, including those drawn upon in this book
such as feminism, neo-Marxist economic theory, and antiracist analy-

ses, are critical of current social arrangements. They seek to demystify how human constructs such as the class, race, and sex/gender systems function so that we can intervene and resist reproducing injustices in our lives. Representing the world from the point of view of subordinate groups, critical forms of social theory help us in the struggle to discern what we need to do to become makers of justice. They help us to critically evaluate our social location so that we, the privileged, can begin to see how we are related to less privileged as well as unprivileged others.[19]

These social theories challenge our social world so that we can act together to reshape it in a way better suited to Christian visions of justice, shared power, and the universal purpose of the earth and its resources. For example, these theories help us see that other people are not simply extensions of ourselves with the same goals and opportunities. Rather, systems of unearned advantage and exclusion separate us into groups with unequal levels of assets (in society's terms) due to our unequal levels of social power. Critical analysis of these systems helps us see how privilege and oppression do not simply coexist side by side. Rather, the suffering and unearned disadvantages of subordinate groups are the foundation for the privileges of dominant groups. The social theories I draw upon help us see that social relations we often take for granted, such as a disproportionate number of people of color in menial jobs and women in charge of housework, are really abusive relations. These commonsense relations involve unshared power, the disproportionate carrying of society's burdens by some groups, and the monopolization of benefits, such as free maid service and more enjoyable, better paid work, by dominant groups.

Social theories that foster this ethical work represent the standpoints of persons excluded from unearned advantage. They often see what is going on in our social systems better than we, the privileged, could ever do by ourselves alone. To study unearned advantage is to stand outside dominant thought patterns and to know something we could not have known without the tools of the outsider's point of view. These interpretations are important, not because they are the only ones, but because they yield alternative perspectives about dominant groups and how social systems work on our behalf. These theories show how the social world is experienced by the majority of people in the world, those who are poor, female, and people of color.

My debt is to the subordinated groups and their allies who have produced such critical social theory and whose knowledge is usually marginalized from mainstream theory, education, and most Christian ethics. My purpose is to explore what we need to know to be moral agents, to gain a perspective on the social relations of advanced white supremacist, male-dominant capitalism, and to become allies with subordinates in strategizing meaningful change.

The Autonomous Self and Invisible Group Power

Why is unshared power taken for granted in our society? One reason that inequality in class, race, and gender power remains invisible is that dominant groups have shaped a cultural ideology, or worldview, based on liberal political theory.

When liberalism analyzes the social world, it focuses on individuals, not social groups. For example, liberal social theory views people who are poor and people who are wealthy as individuals whose different situations are primarily determined by their personal choices and abilities or the effects of random good or bad luck. Affluent and poor groups are not viewed as connected by a common political economy. People in the class system are seen as only accidentally grouped together because of individual choices or unique circumstances. Unlike critical social theory, liberal theory does not acknowledge social power, the power people exercise (or do not exercise) as a result of their group memberships. Nor does it acknowledge a structural relationship between those who enjoy economic, political, and cultural privilege because they are male or white, or have relative economic security, and those who do not.

Liberalism's devotion to the so-called autonomous individual has been dominant in the West since the Enlightenment period of the eighteenth century. In part a response to the constrictions of hierarchical feudal social relations and mean-spirited communal traditions, the myth of individualism inaugurated other kinds of oppressive structures and practices. Emancipation from the control of popes and kings was achieved at the expense of treating others in objective and instru-mental terms. It gave dominant groups, especially the new emerging merchant class, the freedom to economically exploit, politically op-press, and culturally marginalize nondominant groups.

In the United States, subordinate groups such as indigenous peoples, African slaves, and "white savages" or "black" immigrants were "civilized" by being wrenched from their communal settings and turned into an isolated and easily controlled workforce for the busi-ness class. At the same time, the white affluent male whose group monopolized social power was divorced from a communal setting as well. His group created what psychologist Philip Cushman calls a "masterful, bounded, empty self," an identity that was primarily un-derstood in terms of what it was not. The "masterful, bounded, empty self" was *not* the properly subordinated and objectified "other" who was poor, or female, or of color.[20]

Liberal theory has taught dominants that their value lies precisely in not being like others, the actual majority in the world. Subordinate others, on whom dominants depend for labor, entertainment, sexual, and other social services, are thought to need privileged groups to control their lives. Elites consider this arrangement beneficial to both groups. The empty selves of privileged groups, devoid of friendship and community, are then filled up with the services and material goods of consumer society.

Liberal theory ignores the imbalances of power between domi-nant and subordinate groups as it focuses on individuals who enjoy democracy in the voting booth. It is true that the long, slow move out of the feudal world of the sixteenth century into the modern period of the Enlightenment promoted formal political equality for some. This is seen in the eighteenth-century rallying cries of the French Revo-lution, which promoted "liberty, equality, and fraternity," and the American Revolution's famous "liberty and justice for all." However, even though the liberal theory that backed these revolutions was criti-cal of monarchy, feudalism, and a hierarchical view of self and society in the political sphere, modern "democratic" societies rest on a vast network of unacknowledged invisible hierarchies built on the backs of subordinated others.

As I will show in the succeeding chapters, the autonomous public "I" of liberal theory who supposedly enjoys democracy in the political sphere is also a person who occupies the dominant position in the class, race, and sex/gender systems. As political theorist David Harvey says, what is rational for liberal social theory is what is male, white, and economically secure.[21] Ethicist Elizabeth Bounds observes that when we consider how society actually works, privileged groups are hardly autonomous since they are buttressed by an invisible foundation of subordinated "others."[22] These subordinates do the work in so-called private homes and private industries to materially sustain and maintain the public status, lifestyles, and profits of the dominant groups.

People who enjoy economic affluence, especially those who are white, heterosexual, able-bodied, and male, are supported by whole armies of subordinate groups in so-called private homes and workplaces. These groups in the lower sectors of the working class include disproportionate numbers of people of color and white women who build, clean, and service their houses, offices, and vacation spots. These subordinate others make and clean the clothes of the dominant groups; pick, package, and cook their food; clean up their messes; take care of their children; service their cars, planes, appliances, hospitals, and schools; and collect and process their garbage.

Through a regressive tax structure, subordinate groups maintain a disproportionate share of the social infrastructure that sustains us all. If they are not unemployed to keep the general wage level down, these subordinate groups often work at little or no pay with inadequate benefits in order to maintain the political economy within which elites work, play, and accumulate profits. Those in privileged positions in the class, race, and gender systems, however, are taught that their hard work maintains the economy and provides jobs and the good life for everyone else. Because elites have more status and more of the good life than others, they believe this is justly and richly deserved due to their own merits.

In the liberal view of political economy, the home and the business world are thought to comprise the private sector so that domestic and industrial structures are not subject to democratic notions of accountability and shared power supposedly at work in the political sphere.

This private sector work includes the unpaid reproductive and domestic labor of women in the family and the superexploited low-wage labor of subordinate classes, races, and genders in the workplace. It is no wonder that ethicist Jon Gunnemann observes that the autonomous dominant individual of liberal social theory is in reality a parasite.[23]

When privileged groups are inculturated into the ideology of liberal individualism and meritocracy, we are socialized not to see the people whose work maintains our lifestyles or grasp the economic system that gives us access to better jobs and, for a few, stock market profits. Rather, we consider that our work and its opportunity for leisure primarily sustain society. Both before and after the Enlightenment period, traditional ethical discourse has made it seem normal and natural that privileged groups take care of their own needs first so that the rest of society will prosper. This is reflected in the medieval church's view that wealth and social hierarchy are ordained by God for the right ordering of society and the promotion of the commonweal. This is certainly the basis for the acceptance of liberalism in modern Christian ethics, including the legitimation, however qualified, by official Christian bodies of the pursuit of private profit and self-enrichment through the capitalist market.[24] This principle of self-interest is the central concern of liberal economic theory, political democracy, and the philosophy of individual rights.[25]

In the social and economic worlds, liberal theory's view of self and society functions to separate "I" and "others" by the process of objectification. People in dominant groups objectify others, that is, deny them their capacities for self-determination and their rights to shared power in the society. Elites do this in part because they fear losing their dominant position. *Because elites are taught by liberal social theory that they are separate individuals and radically disconnected from others, they fear that others will not be responsive to them. So they use coercive power to make sure their needs will be met.*[26] Coercive power is necessary when autonomy and scarcity and competition, not reciprocity, interdependence, and accountability, are understood to be our fundamental social reality. These notions and practices, which separate us from others and make us feel that we cannot depend on them, breed insecurity and feelings of vulnerability, and insecure people seek to manage and control every aspect of life.

This brings us full circle to the reality that people manage and control others through systems of domination and subordination, especially those of class, race, gender, and sexuality. Subordinates are not viewed as the unique subjects that elites believe they themselves are. Instead, people who are subordinated become objects of imposed definitions so they can meet the needs of insecure elites. These definitions separate others into groups by socially constructed differences, such as class, race, and gender. These socially constructed different identities are often, although not always, tied to physical characteristics, such as skin pigment or reproductive systems, or forms of personal presentation, such as speech or dress. Constructions of class, race, and gender distinguish subordinate groups from dominant groups in order to justify their unequal access to cultural, political, and economic power and their becoming means to the ends of privileged groups.

This "othering" has enormous significance for how we understand our relationships to one another and what is required of ethical persons. Traditional Christian ethics has often assumed that this radical disjuncture between myself and others means that egoism (self-interest) and altruism (other-interest) are opposed. The opposition between egoism and altruism assumes a fundamental disconnection between myself and the social world of others, including human beings, animals, and the biosphere. Either I am focused on myself, *or* I am focused on the other. If I am focused on the other, then I experience doing this at the expense of myself. In addition, when I think of others as radically different from me or separate from me or opposed to me, I can justify their subordination and my privilege. I can also justify my need at times to be altruistic toward others who sometimes need my "help" and are deserving of my self-sacrifice, but never warrant a mutual or reciprocal relationship with me. However, is the self-other split, along with the human-natural world split, an accurate representation of reality?

The Self as a Self-in-Relation

An alternative to liberalism's autonomous and separate "I" is a view of the self as fundamentally in-relation-to-others. We are what we have been able to do (some of us laboring under far more constraints than others) with the cultural ideology, personal relationships, and material structures of our historically specific selves. We are constantly interacting with and mutually reshaping one another, other earth creatures, and the ecosystem itself. What is in the food we eat and the water we drink and the air we breathe is also in us.

In this view there is no radically distinct *ego* whose opposite is *alter*. This view is indebted to social theories that challenge the individualism of liberal social theory. The notion of a fundamentally relational self comes from an analysis rooted in the point of view of those who are located in the subordinate positions of the class, race, sex/gender, and ecological systems. The goal of these theories is to make visible the unacknowledged relations between social groups and between people, other creatures, and the earth. They articulate the perspectives of women of all races, men of color, working-class/working-poor people, and endangered natural systems that are often very clear about the myriad ways that dominant men, whites, and affluent sectors depend on them! An analysis of the privileged individual who is sustained by the invisible labor and resources of others can be unearthed by these social theories. They ground a worldview insisting that there is no autonomous I, that every I exists fundamentally as a self-in-relation.[27]

According to this alternative moral vision, I am radically dependent on all the persons, creatures, and the earth itself who have contributed to my very existence and my continual sustenance in this world. I am a fundamentally social species-being. Who I am is what I have made out of all the social and ecological relations that have impacted me both before and after my birth.[28] The list is endless, but it includes the social relations that have attended to my physical and emotional/spiritual needs and have shaped my political consciousness. It includes my caregivers and all the people, social forces, and material environments impacting them and making it easier, or more difficult, for them to care for me. Since my well-being (or lack thereof) from even before birth is intimately connected to all these humans, creatures, and the earth, what helps them flourish is also good for me.

But interdependence goes farther than this. Not only is our well-being dependent on everyone else's, but we mutually define and redefine one another in unending relational process. Ethicist Elizabeth

Bettenhausen observes, "Because of Holy creativity, all that c‹
tutes the Earth is interdependent—from the wood tick to the blue
whale, from the virus to the mountain. . . . As social creatures we are
not only wholly dependent on the entire planet, but are also always
creating and maintaining each other." Human and nonhuman nature are in constant interaction, mutually shaping and reshaping each
other. "Security on this earth," says Bettenhausen, "is a function of
this interdependence."[29]

This radically relational view of self is the one I assume in this
book. This view is indebted to feminist theorists who have long been
critical of abstract individualism and in various ways richly analyze
the self-in-community. In her review of selected feminist theories,
philosopher Kristin Waters notes that Patricia Hill Collins sees healthy
autonomy as radically dependent upon interconnections. While feminists have called for a woman's right to control what happens to her
physical and emotional self, this is always viewed within a context of
responsible interdependency. In a view that is in harmony with other
feminist approaches, Collins regards an individualistic notion of autonomy not only as inadequate, but as social pathology.[30] This social
pathology is rooted in the dangerous notion that we are fundamentally disconnected from others and must coerce them to get what we
need.

The view of the self as fundamentally relational also converges
with many ancient teachings of this planet's people, including strains
of Taoism, Hinduism, and Buddhism; the mystical teachings of Judaism, Christianity, and Islam; and the worldviews of many indigenous
peoples.[31] The notion of a distinct and separate "I" is not ethically
sound because it conceals the process by which we stand in radical
interdependence and mutual re-creation within an enormous intricate web of social and environmental supports. Since this web is responsible for and necessary to our survival and flourishing, we must
be accountable to it.

Since I as a self-in-relation am in some real sense also a "we,"
ethical relationship, *including the security of all*, requires that all social
groups share cultural, political, and economic power. In this social
theory or worldview, solidarity, not altruism, describes the valued
moral standpoint since no opposition exists between "I" and the "others," between my self-interest and the commonweal.[32] Given the radi-

cal interdependence that is the foundation of our lives and well-being, when I work for the common good, I also work for my own interests. Conversely, without a viable common good, I am in jeopardy. When the air is polluted, when we cannot insure the safety of the global food supply, when there is no tax base to sustain a literate population and a rich culture, when economic restructuring devastates formerly upper-income families, everyone, even privileged groups, suffer.[33] Similarly, when my welfare or the welfare of any other group is at risk, the commonweal suffers since all groups interact to reshape the whole.

Further, if solidarity is a natural capacity of our radically interdependent nature, *solidarity is not something we decide to create so much as it is something we learn to extend.*[34] Social transformation, then, is not a utopian ideal but a viable and necessary moral project. This very project of creating structures to serve the commonweal is not something we need to have imposed from without, but something that emanates from who we are as social beings, radically interdependent on one another and the earth. Moral understanding is learning to uncover and feel bound by the just demands that proceed from our inherently relational nature.

Moral and Political Tasks

The political task at hand, one that is essential to create a moral and secure society, is to fashion a social world that "amplifies benefits and diminishes burdens."[35] It is to fashion a society that can not only feed the hungry, clothe the naked, shelter the homeless, and provide reasonable life chances for everyone, but can also bring community to the lonely, provide meaningful work and play, nurture human creativity, and sustain diverse forms of species life, both in the human community and in the ecosystem.

Many cringe when they hear such a list. Such goals may strike us as naive, if not totally impossible. Because we have been thoroughly indoctrinated with the liberal myth of the autonomous individual competing in the midst of scarcity, we believe that there is not enough—not enough jobs, money, education, health care, or love—

to go around.[36] The analysis contained in this book holds, however, that the only scarce thing is natural resources (which we are told will never run out!). The moral question is, in fact, a political one: How do we transform the structures that mediate our economic, political, and cultural relations so that these goals, grounded in our species-nature, can be better accomplished?

We begin by uncovering and addressing the dynamics of unearned advantage and oppression that are all-pervasive in our society. What must be made visible is how elites stand upon the shoulders of large sectors of subordinated others in the so-called private spheres of home and work. Deepening awareness of our social location is vital in the struggle of privileged people to become ethical. However, since it is also true that we usually lose at least some privileges whenever we resist the status quo, *social commitments even more than social geography determine who we are*. Evaluating how we participate in elite status and what we need to do about it is important work, morally and politically.[37]

Taking responsibility for privilege, letting our social commitments rather than our social geography determine our identity, involves becoming newly accountable to others as we become aware that we are not isolated individuals but selves-in-relation. Exploring systems of monopolized class, race, and gender power helps us to analyze our experiences in relation to pervasive social patterns and systems. According to educator Suzanne Pharr, our personal experiences contain political truth, but we do not comprehend their meaning without the critical information necessary to discern linkages.[38] As we examine the dynamics of systems of class, race, sex/gender, and ecological destruction, we can better discern the specific claims that others may have on us. *Discerning our social location within a web of economic, political, and cultural systems is essential to evaluating our responsibility to others*.[39] It is only at this point that we can start to frame, with others, an ethics of accountability.

Privilege and Christian Ethics

Since the fourth century C.E., the meaning of Christianity has been largely determined by Scripture scholars, theologians, and ethicists from the dominant social groups in the West. Therefore, creating a moral agenda through an examination of privilege has not been a Christian priority. However, since the mid-twentieth century, Christianity's center of gravity has been shifting from the First World to the Two-Thirds World (large sectors of Latin America, Asia, Africa, and growing poor sectors in the First World), not only demographically but also theologically.[40] Since the meaning of Christianity is determined through a dialogue between believers and the historical tradition, and since believers bring to the dialogue concerns from their own social location, subordinated groups are bringing concerns to the dialogue about the meaning of Jesus, Christianity, and ethics that privileged groups have not had. As is true of other forms of cultural perception, those who suffer from poverty, racism, male dominance, and other forms of subordination see things in Scripture and tradition that those who enjoy privilege often miss. For example, liberation theologians with roots in the Two-Thirds World have claimed that salvation in Jesus includes material liberation and freedom from this-worldly oppression as well as spiritual redemption.[41]

As scholars from the overconsuming First World learn from the underconsuming Two-Thirds World, and as new methods of interdisciplinary study help Scripture scholars understand the social world that gave birth to Christianity, emerging work in North America also supports this focus on the material world as a site of redemption. Oppressed Christians in the Two-Thirds World, often working out of movements for their own liberation, and new work by North American scholars on the dynamics of Christian origins are transforming our understanding of Jesus and the movement that became Christianity.

Traditional views of Jesus incorporate notions that he only appeared human and was unconcerned with politics and the social world. For many believers influenced by Western dualistic thought, Jesus has been God who "came down to earth" to ransom individual souls through a historical act of self-sacrificial love. The altruistic ransom that Jesus accomplished is perpetually dispensed to Christians through the sacraments of the church. This view of Jesus did not necessarily challenge the entitlement of the privileged and the suffering of the subordinated because the material world was viewed primarily as a waiting room for the next, and whatever wrongs were experienced here would be corrected in the spiritual world—after death.

Jesus is now understood by an increasing number of Scripture scholars in North America as a radical social critic and a teacher of subversive wisdom.[42] Like many of his fellow Jews who emerged out of the richness of first-century Palestinian Judaism, he challenged a highly stratified society. Jesus, like many Jewish reformers of his day, challenged a society deeply divided between urban elites and the exploited peasantry, polarized by gender and patriarchal family values, and regulated by religious purity laws that legitimated and enforced all the social hierarchies.[43]

This more recently developed view understands that Jesus was crucified because he was passionately involved in the struggle to transform the unjust social world of his day. Therefore, the Jesus movement was a fundamental threat to the status quo. It was not a *political* revolution but a far more radical *social* revolution, a change from the bottom up.[44] Drawn from all sectors of society, the Jesus movement not only preached a new vision. It also lived a confrontational lifestyle, including having open table fellowship with outcasts, touching and healing outsiders, calling religious and political leaders to task, and treating women and slaves as equals. More than annoyances to dominant groups, these behaviors and practices were in fundamental opposition to the religious, cultural, political, and economic hierarchies of the time.[45] They challenged the very foundations of the social order.

Emphasizing the humanity of Jesus, many Scripture scholars and theologians today view him not as an isolated hero, but as one who rode the crest of a wave of renewal in first-century Judaism. Jesus was thoroughly Jewish, and Christians misread him if they do not understand his deep embrace of the Exodus, Jubilee, and prophetic traditions of Hebrew religion. As one shaped by the traditions of his ancestors, Jesus modeled courage in the face of social injustice and invited his followers to live as he did.

The implication for Christians is that we ought not honor respectable hierarchies. The Jesus movement required that people live unconventionally, as though God's reign of radical equality and mutuality had already begun on earth as it is in heaven. Like the prophets of Israel before it, the Jesus movement denounced ideologies and systems that justified and blessed unshared power. It refused to sanction the privilege of dominant political, economic, and religious groups held at the direct expense of others.

In contrast to an older view that Jesus is the exception to the human condition, alternative perspectives understand Jesus as the blueprint for understanding who God is and for understanding who we are.[46] If we wish to better understand what it means to be Christian, we need to look at this outrageous convention-flaunting Jesus movement comprised of folks from both dominant and subordinate groups. People took responsibility for their own power, whether or not it was affirmed in the public sphere. They lived and died in the struggle for the flourishing of all.

As Elisabeth Schüssler Fiorenza writes, *in the process of building a discipleship of equals where there were no excluded ones, the early Christians experienced an extraordinary quality of life for themselves.* In their struggle to break down social barriers between persons and groups and create an alternative community, the fullness of God's life was *"already experientially available"* to them as they were engaged in a this-worldly transformation of social life.[47] Whether rich or poor, slave or free, male or female, Jew or Gentile, they refused to honor conventional social boundaries. They believed that an injury to one was an injury to all and that their concrete commitments in this world, not finally their social location, determined who they were as Christians. The Jesus movement not only critiqued the status quo; it trusted sufficiently in the possibilities of human community that it actually began to embody it.

As contemporary Christians develop a power analysis in order to connect religious norms to a course of ethical practice, we have Scripture as a resource for these norms, and we also have church tradition. One stream in church tradition is modern Catholic social teaching, which includes the documents of bishops and popes that have been periodically issued since the late nineteenth century and address issues of justice, especially economic justice.

Even though some of the social analysis and most of the social policies identified by Catholic social teaching are in harmony with the goals of capitalist liberal society, it is also clear from other strands of analysis and policy prescriptions that this tradition offers a fundamental challenge to economic business as usual. For example, Catholic social teaching has identified values that point to the need for structural change. These include the need for all persons to participate in their society with dignity, the need for democratic values in the economic sphere, the priority of laboring people over the wealth they produce, and the preferential option for a resisting poor who struggle to create new, more just cultural, political, and economic structures.[48] At these points, Catholic social teaching is at home with the ethical sensibilities at the center of Christian origins. This is especially evident in the 1971 document of the World Synod of Catholic Bishops, *Justice in the World*. The bishops challenge "networks of domination" and claim that action on behalf of earthly liberation is at the very heart of the gospel.[49]

Why Christianity Has Avoided Examining Privilege

Despite the above-mentioned resources, Christian ethics, like all symbol systems in the political economy, has been rooted in the material systems of class, race, gender, and sexuality that reproduce inequality. To achieve widespread support, much Christian ethics, like Christianity itself, has not always been faithful to liberation perspectives in its origins or to radical critiques in the subsequent development of its tradition. To be consistent with wider social values, traditional Christian theology and ethics adopted the dualism and hierarchy of the Western philosophical worldview. This worldview predates Enlightenment liberal theory and continues to permeate the cultural, if not the narrowly political values of post-Enlightenment societies. As noted earlier, some strains of Christian theology and ethics have been critical of liberal democratic theory, especially with regard to the unregulated capitalist market.[50] But the majority of Christian teaching has been very much in harmony with the unshared power in family and work arrangements and with the nondemocratic social values that liberal capitalist societies depend upon, but do not acknowledge.

Along with liberal notions of an autonomous self, both philosophical and Christian ethics have supported hierarchies by adopting a metaphysical dualism that conditions people to divide reality into distinct and opposing spheres. One part of the divide is dominant (superior) over the other subordinate (inferior) one. Consequently, Western ethics and the worldview of many people are based on a hierarchical and binary system by which reality is described and values are expressed. Binary opposition is a fundamental process of how Westerners think.

Binary thinking splits the whole person into mind and body and makes the mind dominant. It makes men, whites, Christians, and heterosexuals, for example, dominant over women, people of color, Jews and adherents of other religions, gay people, and the earth itself. These latter are subordinate because, unlike dominants who are identified with the mind and rationality, subordinates are overidentified with their (inferior) bodies, including a deviant sexuality. Binary thinking regards the spiritual realm as dominant over the material earth; it values the eternal as more important than the historical. Binary thinking supports the dominance of church and state authorities over ordinary people, rich people over working-class and poor people, and human beings over other earth creatures and the earth itself. The binary opposites of divine and human have been at the root of doctrinal struggle over who Jesus is. What would it mean for us to consider Jesus (and ourselves) outside binary, hierarchical ways of thinking?

Whenever ethics, including traditional Christian ethics, has been hierarchical and binary, it has operated to support the status quo. For example, Christian ethics has often interpreted Scripture and tradition to affirm the dominant values in the culture. Examples include the consistent theological tradition of ascribing inferiority to people overassociated with their bodies, such as women and Jews. Examples also include the affirmation of slavery by most Christian churches during the centuries of its legalized existence. Still another is the Christian just war theory, which largely operates to affirm the national interests of more powerful states. Ethicist Gloria Albrecht contends that the Christian narrative has always functioned to honor "the master sex, the master race and the master class."[51] We see where this can lead when we look at the Nazi ethic of Aryan supremacy, also rooted in a system of hierarchy and dualism. Deeply indebted to the intellectual history of the West and supported by Christian teaching, Nazism maintained that what is perceived as a threat to the status quo can be justifiably destroyed—primarily Jews but also gays, Gypsies, criminals, and disabled persons.

An Agenda for the Privileged

Not all theology, ethics, and Christian practice have been based on a worldview of binary opposition and hierarchy. As is true in many parts of the world today, there have always been Christians who have joined others in resistance to domination and injustice. Resistance movements demonstrate that those who are subordinates in the cultural, political, and economic spheres are never only victims who suffer domination. They are also people who have enormous creativity and power to resist their subjugation, and they have managed to find resources for their liberatory projects in Christian Scripture and tradition.

Ethics developed from liberatory practice in the social world recognizes that those with monopolized power and privilege are also damaged. The system allows us to be ignorant about subordinates, arrogant in our assumptions about ourselves, and blind to how institutions work on our behalf. We need to explore the impact of internalized oppression on subordinate groups and *the impact of internalized entitlement on dominants.* We need to expose ourselves not only to alternative views about subordinates, but also to new views of ourselves. We need to expose the pathology that comes from enjoying unearned advantage and unshared power at others' expense.

An ethical agenda for people in dominant social locations includes taking responsibility for the beliefs we absorb in an uncritical and unexamined way. These beliefs promote and extend systems of unearned and unshared privilege. An ethical agenda includes taking responsibility for the ways we become (often unwitting) conduits for passing these systems on to others, reproducing and intensifying the monopolization of social power. We need to work hard to break out of our socially constructed identities as class-stratified, male-dominant, white supremacist, and heterosexist people. We need to question our roles in the family, the neighborhood, the church, the workplace, and the political system.[52] The requirements of living an ethical life include being attentive to our particular histories and belief patterns, many of which are explored in the following chapters, that have legitimized our dominant positions and the privileges we receive from them. The moral basis upon which we define ourselves and our relations to one another is the foundation by which we recognize what is just and unjust, what is good and evil.

Taking responsibility for transforming our lives-in-relation requires developing a critical self-consciousness regarding how power operates in society. This challenging, difficult work may produce uncertainty and debate by asking us to leave our comfort zones behind and take on the burdens of "uncertainty, dissension, and critical debate."[53] New ways of seeing and acting involve "crossing borders" as we understand the world and self through the eyes of people we have made "other." This work entails exposing ourselves to a variety of interpretations about ourselves and the way the world works.

Why should we struggle to transform systems of class, race, gender, and ecological destruction? I argue that we do this not only to be just toward others and to insure the planet's very survival, but also to become truly human. As the previous discussion of our radical interdependence suggests, our very capacity to achieve our human/god-like potential is conditioned (and limited) by the larger social collective. Political theorist Stanley Deetz says that our moral agency is challenged when we realize that "the collective is the upper limit of what a person can be rather than the lowest common denominator. The capacity and richness of the individual is limited by the collective capacity—not the other way around."[54] *We can be only as human—as moral—as the communities from which we come.*

We create ourselves through daily social practices received from our society. What kind of selves are being created? What kind of selves do we want to become? What established practices do we want to resist? What new practices need to be imagined, created, and embraced? What kind of people do we want to be, and how do our cultural and religious structures facilitate or frustrate our capabilities of becoming these particular kinds of persons? Isn't this the fundamental moral question: Who will we either willfully or unwittingly become as human beings?

Perhaps most important, we can critically analyze where we have been, what we are now, and who we really want to be only if we have hope for a better way. Hope is perhaps less difficult for subordinates to imagine since they have only their unearned disadvantages to lose. It is more difficult for people in privileged groups since the immediate rewards of unearned advantage from being white or male or heterosexual, or using the earth as a supply house and sewer for economic gain, keep us from seeing our more fundamental moral disfigurement and social peril. We have to work hard to see what others see so easily. To many subordinates, people in dominant positions present themselves as "tiny spirits hiding behind large egos."[55]

When we come to terms with how we are damaged, we can take courage from the fact that, like many in the Jesus movement and in resisting Christian groups throughout history, there have always been people in dominant social locations who have "border crossed." These are people whose moral commitments rather than social geography have defined them. In earlier Christian history, these include renewal movements in monasticism and the Reformation churches. In our own century, these include such movements as Christian-based communities, the Catholic Worker and Sanctuary movements, and Christian support of the labor, civil rights, peace, and feminist movements. Throughout the ages, Christians have insisted that social and economic injustice is a distortion of God's creation and have embraced life-enhancing solidarity.[56] The Christian vocation to justice making requires effective action against systemic, routine injustice and a moral imagination that envisions alternative structures for a better future.

Engaging in critical social analysis, moral imagination, and social action is a challenge for dominants because few of us are encouraged to reflect on the ethical foundations of the society in which we live. However, *without structural analysis, ethical evaluation in light of an alternative vision, and collective action, we risk becoming dangerous conduits of injustice.* After the Holocaust of World War II, philosopher Hannah Arendt recognized "the banality of evil," that is, that very ordinary people could design and execute monstrous deeds on a daily basis.[57] We are susceptible to moral evil when we fail to analyze the social reproduction of misery and injustice through interlocking class, race, and sex/gender systems that regulate almost every dimension of our lives. Since dominant social institutions and cultural practices do not support us in this analysis of preferential treatment for the few, this book will be hard work for most readers.

The work will be difficult because I ask that we think differently about our world and about our place in it. While dominant culture teaches us to individualize and overpersonalize our relationships, I ask that we think about the social groups we belong to and how these groups monopolize the exercise of social power. I ask that we think not only about privilege and social pain, but also about how they are related to each other and what they have to do with us as members of privileged groups.

My goal in this book is to contribute to a process whereby privileged people better understand the social systems that distort and limit our humanity. To call ourselves ethical, we must work in coalition with subordinate others to transform social systems that are detrimental to all. If we are deformed by these systems of privilege and unearned advantage, as I will show, then we can be reformed only by social transformation. This includes being faithful to the liberating vision present in our biblical and church traditions. It includes resistance to these systems collectively as well as in the ordinary daily practices of our personal lives.[58]

However deeply embedded we are in particular social locations of privilege, moral agency first, foremost, and finally depends on the ethical commitments we undertake and the ways we choose to spend our time and material resources. If we come to believe that our humanity is diminished by unfair entitlements, if we believe we have moral obligations to people in other social groups and the earth itself which sustains us, then we can join together with others to resist current social arrangements and to create new ones.

In the chapters ahead I will analyze the race, class, and sex/gender systems with an eye to how they grant routine privileges to elite groups while they also deeply damage elites. As we shall see, the ways class, race, and gender privilege damage elites are legion, but they involve no less than being alienated from ourselves, others, and the natural world. They include being divorced from our own sexuality and playfulness, from our need to deeply trust others, and from our capacities for self-management and creativity. We grow in appreciation for the ongoing personal and moral damage entailed in this state of affairs when privileged people along with others accommodate to such injustice as "the way things are."

In each chapter I will also give account of some resources in the Christian tradition for a moral evaluation of the system in question. In the final chapter I argue that knowledge about the interlocking structure of class, race, and sex/gender systems is essential but not sufficient for ethical response. For this we need a politics of solidarity that has yet to be created and is our ongoing ethical responsibility. In the final chapter I locate support for such a politics in a major discussion of the Christian tradition and the Jesus ethic, as well as in the theoretical work of such ethicists/activists as Janet Jakobsen and Sharon Welch. It is my contention, however, that a politics of solidarity will be possible only when privileged groups understand what is at stake for us in this project. To this work we now turn.

2

Dismantling Whiteness

White people are trapped in a history they do not understand.
—James Baldwin

The race system is a complex web of social institutions that devastates people of color economically, politically, and culturally.[1] The race system, which gives whites dominance over other racialized groups, also restricts whites emotionally and damages us morally. White dominance, or white supremacy, harms people socially constructed as white in ways most whites neither see nor understand. That said, the truth is that whites gain at the expense of communities of color, which is the primary reason for the construction of whiteness and the racial system. Elizabeth Bettenhausen writes that "race is a socially constructed category of power used to create a hierarchy of social relationships that serves the interests of white people."[2]

The effects of white dominance are so pervasive that they can be felt between people of color even when no white people are present, as well as between whites even when no people of color are present. White supremacy includes a color caste system within communities of color and the horizontal violence of people of color because they have internalized this system. White supremacy is at work in whites as emotional reserve and constraint. As we shall see, whiteness is achieved at the expense of internalizing the restrictions required by capitalist work discipline and patriarchal heterosexual domesticity. As a result, white racism, the fallout from the trauma of white racialization, is inextricably linked to attitudes and destructive social patterns that are anti-poor and erotophobic.

Most whites collude with the harm done to us by white racialization because we profit individually and as a group from the system of white dominance. When whites participate in institutions that promote white supremacy, we become deeply shaped by racism.

In this sense, white supremacy is similar to pollution. By participating in white supremacist institutions, we extend white dominance, whether we know it or not, or whether we want to or not. However, as with the problem of environmental pollution, we can do much about white dominance once we study its causes and learn how it works.

A good place to start is to define white supremacy as the act of affirming, going along with, or refusing to recognize "the mechanisms of the white racial state." This definition includes a person's lack of awareness of, or indifference about, being racialized and located within the racial system.[3] The system of whiteness also includes ignorance about how white supremacy works through systems and institutions, not only through personal attitudes and behaviors.[4]

Whiteness is a white problem because white people are the ones who can afford to deny the reality of white racial supremacy. Whites are supposed to ignore the mechanisms of the white racial state while most people who do not have white status are deeply aware of them. Whiteness is also a white problem because the situation of being racially dominant deeply damages whites as it does untold harm to others.

This chapter explores two sets of mechanisms central to the trauma and the overprivilege involved in white racialization. One set generates the social, political, and economic disadvantages for the many and the privilege and unearned advantages for the relatively few who enjoy white racial identity. The other set of mechanisms, which ensues from the emotional restrictions involved in white racialization, generates erotic repression and the denial of the relational self. In short, *whiteness creates unearned advantages at the expense of others while denying dimensions of our relational capacities as human beings.* Otherwise put, the system of white supremacy is compensation for the restrictions involved in white racialization. Whiteness means suffering both moral and emotional damage even as we derive unearned benefits at the expense of others. Defining white supremacy as a refusal to recognize the mechanisms of the white racial state underscores the fact that whiteness is a problematic social construction and institutions in white racist societies promote unearned advantages for whites and erotic regulation for everyone that must be transformed.

Furthermore, this definition moves white supremacy beyond individual acts of discrimination to the fundamental web of complex, interdependent social structures. Institutional patterns constituting the mechanisms of whiteness are pervasive in this society, including the cultural repression and regulation of eros; the racialized labor market; segregated housing, schools, and churches; and the white-controlled media, medical, legal, and other corporate establishments. These reinforce the assumptions that white supremacy is commonsense, while they have devastating material and ideological fallout for communities of color. Whites cannot and will not move effectively against white supremacy until we understand how the fundamental cultural and material structures of society work together to reproduce routine invisible privileges for us and racist outcomes for people of color. These same structures also produce negative emotional, sexual, moral, and spiritual fallout for whites.

This chapter explores the historical creation of whiteness and analyzes how white supremacy is the necessary fallout of white racialization. The methodology here is informed by Christian liberationist perspectives, which affirm that ethical questions deal centrally with power-in-relationship.[5] Unshared power has become commonsense by routinizing the material advantages and cultural dominance of whites as a group. *A historical process has created systems that reproduce monopolized power for whites even as they deny whites access to the erotic, relational self.* While understanding how white supremacy damages whites is a necessary component of Christian antiracist praxis, there are dangers in examining white racial identity. One such danger is the temptation to remain at the level of a theory of white racial identity and white supremacy. However, the goal of antiracist Christian ethics is not only to understand white racialization and white supremacy, but more fundamentally, to dismantle the white system. My thesis is that undoing white dominance will require multiracial, multiclass coalitions to mount a strategic and ethically imperative political response to moral evil.

What Is at Stake for Whites

We do well to investigate white racial identity and the mechanisms of whiteness for at least three reasons. At stake for whites in this project is cultural literacy including increased self-knowledge, responsible agency, and moral integrity as white people.

First, we need to put a spotlight on the history that impacts our daily lives in order to understand what it means to be members of the group known as "white." Whiteness is a major social structure that has developed historically to organize social space and individual experience, including whites' deepest understandings about ourselves and others. When I interact with someone not of my designated racial group, an entire history is embodied between us.

As an example, consider the interchange between an African American woman, Bess Smith, and a white woman, Grace Brown. Bess is a graduate of a historically white college that recently invited alumnae to help organize a women's studies conference at the college. Bess volunteered to organize several panels for the conference, including a presentation of black women poets and a faculty workshop on mentoring women of color. However, Grace and the other white women in charge of this event ignored her requests for information and aid. After many unsuccessful attempts to acquire needed information from the directing committee, Bess wrote a letter to Grace, stating that she was withdrawing her panels from the conference. Bess then received a note from Grace, telling Bess that she was "totally miffed" by Bess's decision.

Reducing this exchange to a personal squabble, as many on the campus did, is predictable if we do not understand the historical dynamics of white racism that have deeply conditioned the relations between black and white women. Many white women do not begin to grasp how white privilege has historically and systemically conditioned their relationships with black women and continues to shape perceptions and daily interactions. Becoming culturally literate requires a more sophisticated analysis of the historical roots and present dynamics of the racial system because this system prevents, or at least frustrates, egalitarian and empathetic relations between women who are racialized differently.

Cultural literacy also demands an understanding of the historical process that confers white status on certain people who relinquished dimensions of their humanity. Historically, white status has been awarded only to those of European background who gave up living close to their bodies and the natural world. As the Industrial Revolution took off in postcolonial America, becoming white was a reward given to those who successfully adapted to a highly regulated and socially repressive capitalist workplace. *Commonsense racism constructs whiteness in order to accommodate the needs of an economic system built upon alienating social and political practices.* As we shall see, in the United States the white self has been created to justify the exploitation of Europeans in industrialized wage labor, and to compensate them for the brutal work discipline that cut people off from their emotions, their sexual desires, and the natural world.

In addition to cultural literacy and self-knowledge, a second reason for whites to explore white racial identity is grounded in the Christian vocation to create a moral world. Whites can discern what is ethical, what we ought to do, only if we listen long and hard to people who endure racism. Christian ethicist Ada María Isasi-Díaz observes that dominants learn what we ought to do as moral agents only by listening to subordinated others and allowing ourselves to be questioned by them.[6] Feminists of color, as well as African American liberation theologians such as James Cone, have persistently called for a critical evaluation of whiteness by whites. During a time of rapid social change at the beginning of the twenty-first century, there is mounting need for whites to become responsible in dealing with increased racial hostility. Listening to and taking seriously people of color will help us see how commonsense racism is pervasive, diffused, and normalized in the culture. Racism is "commonsense" because it is built upon "the norms and forms thrown up by a few hundred years of pillage, extermination, slavery, colonization and neo-colonization."[7]

In learning from people of color we begin to adopt new perspectives about ourselves as whites. Learning to see ourselves from the point of view of the other is the only way to avoid what Iris Marion Young calls the "falsifying projection."[8] She cautions, however, that even with the best of intentions, we can walk in others' shoes *only* as the privileged people we are. As Young insists, in a culture of inequality, we "stand in relations of asymmetry and irreversibility with others."[9] In learning to heed how we misrepresent the disadvantaged situation of others as well as our own advantaged one, we better discern the contours of the moral project. Much of my own critical insight I owe to white Jews and diverse women and men of color who, for centuries, have observed dominants with a critical ethnographic gaze.

Third, repairing white moral integrity is at stake in this project. The system of whiteness has devastating effects upon people of color, and it also supports attitudes, behaviors, and institutions that deeply damage whites and violate our integrity. *Our self-alienation as socially constructed white people lies at the base of our alienation from others.* We need to understand the dimensions of this self-alienation. It is also true that while communities of color have been strengthened by collectively resisting the racialized system, the moral integrity of whites is eroded by our continuing efforts to benefit from injustice. Therefore, white racial identity bestows unearned advantages, and it damages its supposed beneficiaries. The fundamental moral project for whites is doing the work necessary to recover integrity by dismantling the white system.

The Dangers of Exploring Whiteness

On the one hand, white people need to be weaned from our attachment to white privilege and the white supremacist construction of our identities. On the other hand, confronting whiteness can have deleterious effects. These hazards include guilt, hopelessness, self-absorption, and confusion about our capacity to be allies in antiracist work.

White people are tempted to guilt and/or hopelessness when we learn about the enormity of the racialized system and how it privileges and disables us as it disadvantages and oppresses others. Being embarrassed and feeling shame may be good insofar as they maintain our moral bearings and prompt us to develop a positive agenda for change. However, because people often feel hopeless about a legacy over which they seem to lack control, many whites become morally evasive about racial identity and escape into other aspects of social location, such as being female, gay, or Jewish.

Here clarity about blame and responsibility is needed. No one alive today is directly to blame for creating the racial system. Yet my family has been able to take for granted things that others might never have access to at all. While we are not responsible for the historical creation of racism, the fact that we systematically benefit from this inherited system that simultaneously disadvantages others marks the location of our personal accountability.

Perhaps the worst danger in becoming preoccupied with whiteness is that we can become self-absorbed and kept from crafting an antiracist political agenda in coalition with others. Therefore, the message cannot be repeated too often: the solution to white supremacy is not guilt, hopelessness, or self-absorption. Rather, the solution is the democratic appropriation of economic, political, and cultural power, which can be forged only by the hard work of coalition politics. What is needed is a politics centered on making connections across differences, a coalition politics of resistance and solidarity across racial/ethnic lines. Simply put, although we cannot help accidents of birth, we can do something about the way we spend our time, energy, and money.

In the search for a viable antiracist politics, whites have much work to do. We need to gain a clearer sense of how we have been racialized, how we define and enforce social categories connected to race, and how some receive more unearned advantage from whiteness than others. For example, the experience of whiteness is significantly different for a working-class lesbian and an affluent heterosexual male. It is qualitatively different for a Christian and a Jew—who sometimes benefits from white privilege but is also the target of anti-Semitism. Although class, gender, ethnicity, religion, and sexual orientation change qualitatively the experience of white supremacy, *it is also true that, to greater or lesser degrees, virtually all whites now benefit from white supremacy.*[10] In every social location whites have work to do because we have only begun to listen to the analysis of racially subordinate others, the only way to demystify whiteness and its legacy within us.[11]

One way to take inventory of whiteness is to analyze how the white system provides a twofold function for people socially constructed as white. First, whiteness provides psychological compensation for capitalist exploitation and the rigors of adhering to industrial morality and patriarchal domesticity. Second, whiteness provides concrete material rewards through a system of affirmative action for whites in the economic, political, cultural, and ecological spheres. This system is invisible to whites but blatantly evident to communities of color.

Whiteness as Wages for Industrial Morality

White racial identity has been historically constructed and reproduced in Western societies through cultural patterns anchored in the material institutions of capitalist political economy. Even though whiteness is customarily associated with skin color, whiteness is first and foremost a social construction. Historically, not all light-skinned people have been accorded white status. A historical analysis shows that whiteness is not primarily related to skin pigment, but is a cultural creation that serves vested interests.

Scholars have argued that white racial identity in the United States is rooted in the search of exploited European workers for economic advantage and cultural status. For example, historian Noel Ignatiev argues that the social construction of whiteness was a response to the need of nineteenth-century immigrant workers, especially the Irish, to disassociate themselves from the exploitation and oppression of slavery. After years of competing with "free" blacks for the worst jobs, the "black" Irish gained the right to become "white" by joining other European immigrant groups in excluding black workers from most industrial employment.

Forced to sell themselves piecemeal to the nineteenth-century factory owner, these workers sought to salvage their self-esteem by distinguishing themselves from former slaves. Workers accomplished this by establishing segregated unions, thereby rendering most forms of industrialized labor as white preserves. In this way, white workers tried to convince themselves that if blacks were excluded from certain forms of labor, the demeaning work they endured was not actually wage slavery. Selling oneself piecemeal became dignified (white) work if people of European origin were the only ones allowed to do it. Ignatiev argues that the very construction of the U.S. working class depended on the construction of whiteness, such that "the distinction between those who did and those who did not have access to the most dynamic area of the economy became a principal element defining 'race' in the North."[12]

While Ignatiev focuses on the type of labor monopolized by groups constructed as white, historian David Roediger focuses on the cultural characteristics required of workers in a white-only industrial workplace. Notions of whiteness are rooted in the industrial morality of hard work, self-discipline, and strict sexual regulation required by the long hours, intense supervision, and uninterrupted pace of capitalist work. To survive a brutalizing, unstable economy, industrial workers who had recently been torn away from agrarian life rejected preindustrial patterns of being human. Among these norms were being in touch with the erotic, including nature's rhythms and one's own sexuality, and being able to enjoy a more simple, carefree, and noncommercialized style of life.[13]

The construction of blackness—and racism—is the other side of socially constructed whiteness. Deprived of relationship to the land and access to the natural world, and subjected to extremely routinized work, rural-born immigrants were shoved into densely populated urban slums and dangerous, overcrowded factories. Their anxieties due to severed relationships with nature, leisure, and their own bodies were projected onto people vested with blackness, who came to be perceived as oversexed and irresponsibly playful. The social construction of white and black created a relationship of fascination and repulsion, of longing for what was lost and hatred for the preindustrial (black) self.[14]

Both Roediger and psychologist Philip Cushman agree that minstrel shows and whites' appearing in blackface were tools in the creation of whiteness. These popular theatrical forms were developed by Europeans frustrated by the enormous social dislocations of industrialization. Minstrelsy and blackface allowed an angry, exhausted working class, as well as the prim-and-proper Victorian entrepreneurs, to indulge in and mockingly reject the "black" part of themselves that loved music, dancing, clowning, relaxing, and sex.[15] A new industrial morality of whiteness, imposed on upper and lower working class sectors alike, was constructed over against the blackness of the "savage, lazy, sexual, communal" American Indian, the enslaved or free Negro, and the newer European immigrant.[16] As a component of a more expansive racist folklore about the lazy, erotic, careless, and carefree black, these cultural forms of minstrelsy and blackface allowed people with white status to indulge at least momentarily in these longed-for attributes and escape the harshness of their lives. Like Ignatiev, Roediger argues that the even more exploited black other

allowed those with whiteness to sublimate their own economi
ploitation and social oppression. Like Cushman, Roediger argues that
whiteness developed as a disciplined industrial morality and held together diverse immigrant groups in a relatively homogenized but
empty capitalist culture. White racist capitalism has required sexual
and social regulation, and has placed in opposition those who at-
tained whiteness and those who were excluded.[17]

Critical theorist Herbert Marcuse shows how industrial morality
intensified its authority in the twentieth century. In his analysis of the
social controls of modern industrial society, Marcuse argues that
preindustrial characters who were noncompliant and disruptive, such
as the artist, adulteress, rebel-poet, and the fool, were replaced in the
new technological world. Their successors are freaks, such as the beat-
nik, the neurotic housewife, and the gangster. These character-roles
do not challenge the intensified social control of industrial society.[18]
Disruptive figures who once helped people imagine an alternative to
the status quo have been deprived of any antagonistic force by being
made into commodities that are sold everywhere and incorporated
into everyday reality.[19] Using Marcuse's analysis, one could argue that
in this century, the social creation of whiteness also co-opts and
trivializes images of other ways of life and thereby makes unimagin-
able the rebellion these alternative images imply.

I think it is important for whites to recognize that white racial
identity is an identity created and sustained under duress. Achieving
white status requires people to adopt the "personal rigidity, loneli-
ness, isolation, and lack of imagination, humor and creativity" necessary to function in the technologized workplace.[20] It requires isolated,
predictable personalities who perpetrate killings in the market, in the
concentration camp, and on the battlefield. As Scripture scholar Walter
Brueggemann observes, people fully accommodated to the social controls of technologized capitalist society can implement almost anything and imagine almost nothing.[21]

In the process of becoming white, whites have lost access to themselves. For example, white people have had to become numb to the
suffering within and around them. They have learned to divorce
themselves from their bodies and to despise what is particular to all
human beings, vulnerability and mortality. They have learned to deny

their physical and sexual needs. White culture supports contempt and outrage for children, poor people, disabled persons, and those overidentified with their sexuality, who seem unable to keep their needy bodies under strict control. In adopting a white industrial morality, people constructed as white have split off fundamental aspects of their humanity, especially their capacity for relationships. These aspects have been demonized and shunted onto black (Negro, American Indian, Irish, Chinese, Latino, Jew, etc.) others who are characteristically portrayed as oversexed, carnal, lazy, and irresponsible. Blackness embodies preindustrial ways of being human and the desire for leisure time and pleasures from nature and from a more spontaneous sexuality that whiteness considers uncivilized.

However, blackness must be demonized precisely because a white capitalist political economy cannot accommodate these human traits and desires within the constricted parameters of capitalist culture. Profits go down without desexualized bodies as instruments of labor and profit making. Profits go down when people can do without products to correct the deficiencies of inadequate bodies and repressed sexuality. Profits go down if people are not highly regulated and obsessed with work. Profits go down if the black erotic is not rechanneled into the service of capitalist work, the reproduction of *new workers, in heterosexual domesticity,* and selling products.[22] At the same time, aspects of the white self that are no longer acceptable are deeply grieved and longed for, as well as hated and scorned.[23] To become white, people divorce themselves from what feels right and good to them and lose their ability to imagine an alternative future. A white student observed, "When you analyze white people from this point of view, you can really feel sorry for us."

As Roediger argues, the social construction of whiteness over against a scapegoated black other has been essential to the stability of capitalism. The scapegoating of blacks requires most people of color to be more exploited and oppressed than most whites. If the situation of communities of color improved substantially, or if social systems such as authentic welfare reform gave some relief from economic misery, the vast majority of whites could no longer ignore their own suffering through class exploitation.[24] Both Ignatiev and Roediger draw on a wide variety of scholarship to support W. E. B. DuBois's insight that degraded and superexploited workers of color have always been necessary to bolster white workers who cash in on "the psychological wages of whiteness."[25] Whiteness has cushioned workers against their hatred of capitalist work discipline and eased their fears about their dependence on wages. In so doing, the racial system has divided and conquered the majority of workers who sell their productive abilities for a wage.

In a similar vein, with today's increasing numbers of low-wage workers and people's escalating fears around job security, many workers distinguish themselves as reliable, responsible, and indispensable workers in contrast to the despised welfare recipient, largely perceived as a nonworking woman of color. Social theorist Ann Withorn notes that, as more people work harder under deteriorating conditions in the labor force, the thought of others collecting money without having to endure similar immiseration has become an increasingly hot zone for people. As more people endure abusive marriages and take on multiple jobs that make them sick and deprive them of time with their children, the fear that others might have some alternatives to these situations raises questions about the value (and necessity) of their own suffering.[26] The emotional volatility around welfare recipients is not about the recipients, but about the compromises that whites have been told they must make to survive, compromises that whites deeply resent.

Making Whiteness Divine to Increase White Wages

Because white status is bought at such a great price, whites try to increase the psychological wage by scapegoating others and divinizing whiteness. As we have seen, white dominance is rooted in the need to split off the vulnerable and dependent self onto racialized and impoverished others. Such marked others assuage the emotional needs of suppressed, angry whites by offering them scapegoats as well as subordinates to care for them or entertain them. Instead of facing their own exploitation and struggling to overcome white oppression in the social order, whites intensify scapegoating. This practice uses others not only to restore faith in the goodness of whites, but also to mitigate whites' own suffering.

White people's need to dominate the racialized other has survived desegregation, affirmative action, and visions of racial equality, goals that a few decades ago seemed in sight. Rooted in whites' oppression, this need to dominate others is reinforced by grandiose views of white people. These views are so strong that many, perhaps most, whites believe that others view them as paragons of virtue. Whites believe that others view them as virtuous and pure rather than dirty (whites do not do their own cleaning), as kindly rather than cruel (whites kidnap people for slave ships and ovens).[27] Whites believe that whereas communities of color speak from a narrow, culturally biased viewpoint, they themselves speak from a universal, unbiased viewpoint. White morality grants sympathy to victims but never redress or reparations to equals.[28] White morality presumes that white people are not prejudiced, that they have earned their way through individual merit, and that being ethical requires following the forms, procedures, and due process within social systems created by powerful whites.[29] Manning Marable adds that white religion "provides an intellectual shield through which the oppressive essence of their economic and political systems are made virtually invisible."[30]

In light of this analysis, it is easy to see why "the habit of whiteness and the conditions producing it have survived."[31] For whites to construct an identity outside the racist construct, we would need to give up our socially constructed white selves and embrace the rejected parts of our humanity that require scapegoats. Whites would need to give up proving ourselves on the terms required by capitalist political economy. Whites would challenge the belief that it is virtuous to be body denying, desexualized, and work obsessed. Challenging industrial morality means questioning a work ethic that says it is honorable to work multiple jobs even though the wages earned can never raise one's family above the poverty line. Challenging escalating economic insecurity would require honesty about the fact that it is less than just that one can hold a relatively good job now, but cannot count on holding it in the future. Whites would need to give up the self-righteous claim that because we work hard on capitalism's terms, so should everyone else. Instead of seeking to achieve status from white capitalist morality, whites would have to challenge the rigidly moralistic class, race, and sexual system. *Rather than being superaccommodating*

to the political economy and its institutions, whites would instead acknowl-edge that we deserve better, and so does everyone else.
    In short, change would become possible only by shattering people's psychic and spiritual numbness to the misery within and around them. Change becomes possible only when whites can mourn the alienation from self and others that is the foundation of whiteness. However, given all the functions whiteness continues to serve, one scholar writes, "If race lives on today, it does not live on because we have inherited it from our forebears . . . but because we continue to create it today."[32]

The existence of even more impoverished and culturally marginal communities of color has been necessary to stabilize a system that has guaranteed whites some measure of ideological and material compensation for their self-alienation in this political economy. Racist practices are even more necessary to maintain the current status quo as whites' needs are increasingly subordinated within the larger political economy, which demands self-negation from most citizens, whites as well as people of color.

Invisible Affirmative Action for Whites

The wages of whiteness are not only psychological; they are also material and concrete. In addition to providing emotional compensation for the suffering involved in being faithful to industrial morality, whiteness provides invisible affirmative action for whites in the economic, political, cultural, and ecological spheres. A second major feature of whiteness is its unequal access to power, privileges, and benefits in all sectors of the society. Whiteness is a vast invisible system of affirmative action for whites, although truthfully speaking, what may be invisible to us may be very visible to communities of color. As Paul Kivel notes, the entire system of whiteness is maintained "to construct a normative set of values which defines who is entitled to certain resources and privileges," who is denied access, and who is scapegoated for social problems.[33]

The racial system accomplishes this by homogenizing people within groups and establishing a hierarchy of absolutely distinct human populations. However, the historical process of race making is unstable because groups are not homogeneous, and more overlap than difference exists between racialized groups. White supremacy is, in part, an effort to undermine the commonalities among peoples whose differences must be exaggerated if some groups are to maintain unfair advantage. White dominance in the political, economic, and cultural spheres denies that the various communities of color are as diverse as whites and, equally telling, that they share commonalities overlapping with whites.[34]

On the individual level, educator Peggy McIntosh describes white affirmative action as an invisible package of unearned assets that whites cash in daily, but about which we are meant to remain oblivious.[35] These privileges include not living in fear for our own or our children's safety, having greater access to better jobs and educational institutions, receiving fair representation in the media and the court system, being assumed to be financially reliable in business transactions, and having social permission to be ignorant of other people's cultures.[36] When those without these race-based advantages fail to measure up to white standards, they are then penalized and required to bear a greater share of society's burdens while simultaneously receiving unequal access to society's benefits.

On the institutional level, the system of routinized unfair advantages in favor of whites means that the absence of overt discrimination will not, by itself, make up for unequal schools, redlined neighborhoods, segregated job markets, and exclusionary banking and housing policies. A lack of overt discrimination by individuals will not compensate for unfair treatment by theological doctrines, the media, the medical and legal establishments, or the criminal justice and social welfare systems. *Institutionalized racism means that visible affirmative action for individual people of color is a drop in the bucket compared to the pervasive, yet unacknowledged, affirmative action for whites as a group, in every dimension of the political economy.*

Accurately drawing a picture of affirmative action for whites requires unpacking white racial advantage as it is manifested in economic and political privilege, cultural hegemony, and ecological apartheid. The following brief inventory uncovers only the tip of the iceberg, but it may identify pressure points to be targeted by coalition work in dismantling whiteness and building a more just, antiracist society.

Economic Affirmative Action for Whites

In differentiating whites from superexploited others, the system of white racial identity also secures economic advantage for whites. As we have seen, white supremacy has created and historically maintained systematic inequalities in work and in meeting material needs in order to compensate for the economic struggle of most whites in the class system.

Whiteness, however, keeps most whites ignorant of the fact that the very existence of communities of color in the United States is due to conquest, colonialism, and the deliberate importation of cheap labor for purposes of profit making for whites. A primary example is that, as a group, African Americans have perhaps paid the highest price in their service to the evolving U.S. economy. They have worked as slaves, forced breeders of slaves, and sharecroppers, and more recently, they have been disproportionately represented at the lowest rungs of industrialized labor, including prison labor and the unemployed.[37]

African Americans are not alone in overserving the economy. In the mid-nineteenth century, Spanish-speaking peoples entered the United States in large numbers as their homelands were colonized by U.S. forces expanding markets for U.S. business. In addition, American business recruited Chinese to help replace abolished slave labor. More recently, Latino/as have arrived to serve the need for labor in the Southwest as a result of the U.S. blockade of Cuba, interventions in Haiti, and U.S.-sponsored dictatorships in Central America and South America.[38]

A current example of the exploitation of immigrants by (mostly white) stockholders is the U.S. meat-packing industry, which depends largely on Laotian and Chicano workers. These immigrants are recruited, exploited, and exhausted in dangerous jobs that are typically sustained for less than a year. When workers are let go or suddenly expelled by the U.S. Immigration and Naturalization Service (INS), their employers avoid having to pay health benefits. In this way, the INS keeps labor transitory and invisible, and industry is guaranteed an inexhaustible supply of impoverished workers of color.[39]

A historical analysis of labor markets makes clear that whites collectively enjoy much of the capital accumulation, infrastructure, agriculture, food processing, child care, housecleaning, cooking, and basic maintenance of the society that has been disproportionately performed by slave labor and low-wage labor of men and women of color. Granted, whites have also worked hard, but they have had access to schools and universities, school loans, VA loans, housing and auto loans, unions, job contracts, and farming programs, all of which have excluded peoples of color and sometimes white Jews as well.[40] White dominance has built a global capitalist system through the disproportionate labor of workers of color and their children, who have been superexploited through the systems of slavery, colonialism, neocolonialism, and now the intensified system of global low-wage labor, which is deepening even in the United States.

Another way the race system maintains the economic status quo is the use of "the race card" to conceal class analysis and the overlap in the impoverishment of poor and working-class whites alongside communities of color.[41] At the beginning of the twenty-first century economic vulnerability is the lot of increasing numbers of people across the color line. Whiteness no longer protects the way it once did. Consequently, those at the top of the economic hierarchy find racism especially important in maintaining the status quo. Promoting hostility between racial groups keeps white workers and workers of color divided, both nationally and internationally. Even as they share common positions at the bottom of the economy, their lack of unity promotes the smooth functioning of the global economy.

Finally, while it is true that the subordination of people of color within the workplace is a significant dimension of white dominance, class relations do not exhaust racism. For example, in apartheid South Africa, the "color bar" at times was allowed to inhibit profit making. When making maximum returns for investors collided with the apartheid system, the whites in charge of the economy tolerated a latitude of inefficient operation. In order to maintain white supremacy, they even worked against their immediate economic interests.[42]

Cultural Affirmative Action for Whites

White cultural affirmative action requires that white language, values, images, history, literature, music, and religion are constantly reflected as normative to everyone in the society. At the same time, whites expropriate the culture of racialized others by distorting, packaging, and marketing whatever cultural elements suit the purposes of white pleasure, profit, and escape from the repression and boredom of whiteness.[43] As the primary shapers and beneficiaries of a bureaucratic and hierarchical culture of consumption, affluent whites decontextualize other cultures, which are then consumed as exotic. In the process, whites are guaranteed not to be confronted or changed by an encounter with the other.[44]

At the same time that the white system consumes the culture of others, it uses the media and other white cultural forms to scapegoat the people to whom these cultures truly belong. A politics of representation blames peoples of color rather than the U.S. system of white supremacist inequality for our culture of violence. For example, television programs and movies blame Asian American and Jewish economic success, as well as African American poverty, for the troubles experienced by poor and working-class white people.[45] In this way whites objectify and define the other as the source of societal ills rather than as the primary recipients or, more significantly, as resisters of the violence created by white capitalist society. The process of scapegoating keeps whites from paying attention to the source of their own exploitation and oppression.

Political Affirmative Action for Whites

Political power is monopolized by whites, who are elected by those who control the economic and cultural spheres. In the political sphere, white supremacy means that public policy is often intentionally coupled with a racially charged perspective in order to gain support for the policy and elicit the collusion of whites across class lines.[46] For example, although more people on welfare are white rather than African American, policy for dismantling welfare is racially coded so that the typical welfare recipient is inaccurately portrayed as a black woman.[47] Most illegal drugs are manufactured and sold by whites, and more than three out of four drug users are white, accounting for 80 percent of cocaine consumption. However, white supremacist criminal justice policy places predominantly poor people of color in jail for drug use.[48]

White political hegemony is further illustrated when nondominant groups attempt to focus public attention on their concerns, but whites steal the center. For example, when white women equate sexism with racism, gender oppression typically receives center stage. The experiences of women of color are rendered invisible, as illustrated in the Anita Hill–Clarence Thomas televised hearings. Many white feminists assessed the problem as sexual harassment "pure and simple," and yet many African American women recognized a more complex and familiar white-racist drama. As noted earlier, the social construction of whiteness involves oversexualizing black women and men. For many people of color, the Hill–Thomas hearings were spectacles for whites to project their fears, fantasies, and repressed desires onto scapegoated blacks.[49]

These insights are difficult for many whites to assimilate, especially if they do not comprehend the mechanisms of the white racial system. Similarly, Ida B. Wells, a nineteenth-century social reformer, observed that white women did not recognize lynching as a feminist issue because they did not understand their white-racist participation in the oppression of black men. Today, few white feminists understand why antirape "Take Back the Night" campaigns also require efforts to oppose disproportionately severe criminal sanctions, including stiffer prison sentences, for men of color.[50]

Knowledge of white political oppression is also necessary to make sense of the interchange cited earlier between Bess Smith and Grace Brown. White women, for example, are often less aware than black women of how white women have occupied the roles of both economic exploiter and political oppressor in relation to black women. Interactions between black and white women are never free of the history of black women as slaves and servants to white women. Neither are they free from more recent patterns of servitude in which white women have built professional careers from the subsidies provided by the low-wage labor of women of color in white homes in white factories across the globe. Interaction between Bess Sn.... and Grace Brown is not free of the history of betrayal that women of color suffered in the women's suffrage movement because of white women's refusal to take women of color seriously as equal partners. Because this sordid history shapes white women's perceptions of black women and vice versa, it is no surprise that black women have reason not to trust us.

Understanding the mechanisms of the white racial system helps white women see that comparing race and gender oppressions is highly suspect, although whites often do so. By claiming others' experience as our own, we do not have to comprehend their actual experience or be fully accountable to it.[51] Deepening our understanding of the mechanisms of white racism helps white women respond to bell hooks's insight that "as long as white and black women are content with living separately in a state of psychic social apartheid, racism will not change."[52] As the interchange between Bess and Grace illustrates, however, white women will not be ready for solidarity until we learn from black women, including how not to crumple in the face of conflict.[53]

Another way whites avoid coming to terms with other groups' experiences is often through political language about multiculturalism. The rhetoric of multiculturalism may be popular, in part, because it lumps all communities of color together so that whites are not required or expected to take seriously each group's specific claims. It allows whites to construct an imaginary symmetry in which all races "appear and are treated as though they occupy a *common* position in relation to each other and the state."[54] The racist absence of shared power, which gives rise in the first place to the need for multiculturalism, is never addressed.

Ecological Affirmative Action for Whites

The construction of whiteness results as well in ecological alienation and insensitivity to nature and its rhythms. White elites monopolize the use of land and natural and human resources while destroying the earth and its atmosphere. The long-term consequences of environmental destruction will, of course, be fatal for all. In the meantime, ecological affirmative action for whites means that communities of color (and poor nations) are more likely than affluent white areas to be sites of pollution production and hazardous waste facilities. Geographer Joni Seager writes that "race is one of the most significant variables in determining the location of commercial, industrial and military hazardous waste sites."[55]

For example, south-central Los Angeles, 59 percent African American and 38 percent Latino, is the dirtiest community in the state with more than 33 million pounds of toxic waste dumped there in 1989.[56] Similarly, major hazardous waste sites in the nation include Sumter County, Alabama, and the southeast side of Chicago, which also have predominantly African American and Latino populations.[57] In addition, the greatest producer of toxic waste is the military whose nuclear bomb testing sites in the continental United States are all located on Native American lands, mostly on Shoshone territory in Nevada.[58] *While more than half the U.S. population currently resides in areas with uncontrolled hazardous waste sites, communities of color are predominantly targeted.* This is true both in the United States and in the Two-Thirds World, demonstrating continuing patterns of imperialism, colonialism, and racism.[59] As a result, children of color suffer disproportionately from lead levels in the blood, respiratory diseases, cancer, and other health problems. It is no surprise that primarily men and women of color and white women, understanding the connections between poverty, racism, and sexism, are leaders in the struggle for ecological justice.[60]

Moreover, the white supremacist global economy creates both the degradation of poverty and the assault of affluence. Each threatens the earth's life-support systems, though in exceedingly different ways. White supremacy will not protect even whites, for as Larry Rasmussen warns, "If this situation continues, we will not."[61]

How Whites Are Hurt by White Privilege

While hardly suffering the devastating costs that accrue to diverse communities of color, whites bear significant economic, emotional, and spiritual suffering because of the white system we have been carefully trained to accept as normative. What costs do whites bear? Consider the following:

As previously mentioned, whites suffer alienation of the white self from the erotic, including the divorce from the natural world, from one's own sexuality, and from spontaneity, playfulness, and creativity. The system of whiteness restricts and constrains our relations with other white people. Capitalist culture and its system of profit making cannot accommodate people having access to their full selves for fear they will become assertive about what feels right and good to them. Perhaps most sobering of all, white alienation from ourselves and others lies at the origin of our alienation from nature as planetary destruction threatens the sustainability of all life-forms.

Whites suffer arrogance in believing that knowledge, including moral knowledge acquired through a white racial lens, is the measure of all things. We also live with an inaccurate picture of history and politics, including ignorance of the crimes and practices of white people.

Whites are hurt by our outstanding ignorance about the white racialized state and how our systematic unearned advantages permeate every aspect of our lives. Ignorance of the historical record, including how white people have betrayed people of color, is central to failed communication, which frustrates coalition work.

And how do we begin to calculate the loss to society of the contributions of communities of color, had they not been burdened with systematic unearned disadvantage and oppression? Equally painful is the loss of our own ethnic cultures insofar as white racial identity is defined over against the racialized other who embodies all that must be rejected from the self as white.

Whites are hurt, too, by the lack of friendship and intimacy that capitalist culture inflicts on people in order to sell products that appeal only to those who are insecure in community life. Whites suffer the loss of friendship with people of color in our largely segregated lives. A related problem is the confusion and helplessness whites feel when confronted by angry people who do not share white privileges. White racism disempowers whites by blocking us from the increased power we would gain in forging alliances with communities of color.

In addition, whites sometimes lose the friendship of other whites, even in our own families, in confrontations over racism. We are taught to live in fear of people of color, although they are the ones at risk from white supremacy. If we are not wealthy, we remain ignorant about our own exploitation by (Christian) whites who control the economy and teach us to blame economic troubles on Jews and people of color. If we are women, we remain ignorant about the real source of personal violence in our lives, which is white men we live with or near, not the stranger of color.[62] White privilege ensconces whites in immaturity and incompetence. From their vantage point as servants, black women have often regarded white women collectively as "willful children, pretty children, and mean children," but not as very competent.[63]

Perhaps most important, white privilege leads to moral bankruptcy. Because white status depends on denying the deepest parts of the relational self, our humanity is impoverished, and our capacity to be moral—in right relationship with others—is diminished. White supremacy produces trauma, pain, fear, ignorance, mistrust, and unshared vulnerability, and for this reason, white moral character is warped and undermined.[64] Our integrity is necessarily damaged in environments that systematically promote discrimination, harassment, exploitation, and misery. Our integrity is damaged when, as participants in white culture, we are divorced from our deepest longings and capacities for creativity, and when we do not know how to intervene.[65]

White people purchase hegemonic power at the price of splitting off aspects of our authentic humanity, including our vital human need for mutual recognition and respect. In different ways everyone is assaulted, wounded, and deformed by the process of being racialized. Racialization denies our commonalities, and in the process we cut ourselves off from others. The tragedy here, as African American writer Barbara Smith points out, is that integrity of character, including moral insight and action, can come only from emotional and spiritual connection.[66]

The ethical goal of mutual recognition and shared power will not be achieved until white people understand the damage done to whites by the historical process of being racialized as white. The Boston-based Combahee River Collective says it well: "The most profound and potentially most radical politics comes directly out of our own identity, as opposed to working to end somebody else's oppression."[67]

Catholic Social Teaching and Racism

Catholic resources for addressing racism are exceedingly limited, in large part because of the racist practices of the church itself. The Catholic Church has a racist history that, along with racist U.S. society, continues to impact its organizational structures and the individual attitudes of most Catholics. This history includes (but is not exhausted by) the theological justification of slavery; the ownership of slaves; complicity in the mistreatment and genocide of American Indians; refusal to let people of color into the priesthood, religious life, and parish and diocesan leadership positions; participation in legal segregation and white flight; marginalizing Catholics who participated in the civil rights movement; the direction of church resources to suburban rather than urban areas; and the failure to teach its official stand against racism in schools, seminaries, parishes, and the public arena.[68]

The official stand of the church against racism has been made especially explicit in the U.S. bishops' 1979 pastoral letter, *Brothers and Sisters to Us*.[69] While some critics wish the bishops had detailed a more thorough structural and theological analysis of racism, this document offers resources to those concerned with dismantling whiteness.[70] The bishops write that racism distorts the personhood of whites by its promotion of indifference and resentment.[71] But racism not only characterizes individuals; it is deeply embedded in society's institutions and organizations. The bishops are clear that racism systemically reproduces unearned advantages for whites and unearned disadvantages and suffering for people of color when they state that society's institutions "are geared to the success of the majority and the failure of the minority."[72] *The bishops exhort Christians to learn how social structures reproduce white supremacy and how the church has directly participated in racism.* The bishops then outline specific strategies in which Christians and their churches can engage, including expanding the participation of people of color at every level of church life through a more rigorous application of affirmative action than is evident in secular institutions.[73]

Brothers and Sisters to Us was written more than twenty years ago and has been reaffirmed in other Catholic documents.[74] Nevertheless, the Catholic position on racism is little known, and most of its policy prescriptions have never been implemented. Especially unconscionable is the largely unheeded mandate to publicly confess past and present wrongs, express contrition for them, and actively work to make amends.

Given this sad track record, it is clear that the church first needs to work hard on its own racism. Only then will its call to dismantle racism and white supremacy in the larger society have any impact. Working against its own racism will also entail joining with others in organizing and implementing concrete policies and structures to address racist violence, police brutality, economic exploitation, homelessness, hunger, and unequal access to education and health care. To be effective in dismantling white supremacy, the churches need to transform their own institutional practices and ally themselves with others in the larger work of antiracist coalition politics.

Dismantling Whiteness through Coalition Politics

The institutional churches, like individual Christians, can work to understand the racial system and join with others in the project of dismantling white racialization and white privilege. While we do not choose our racial location, we can take charge of our political actions out of the knowledge that justice benefits everyone, at least in the long run. Our shame about the truth of white supremacy will not immobilize whites if, through a shared analysis of racialized power and how it works to hurt most people in this society, we can identify common benefits. It will be clear how each of us will gain through investments of time, energy, and risk taking required in solidarity work.[75] When we analyze the system of white supremacy and understand how it is built on the trauma of white racialization and both reinforces and is supported by other processes of domination that hurt most whites as well, it becomes more evident how diverse coali-

tion partners can have their interests met by a comprehensive a
of the status quo.[76] This precursor to systemic change is located in the
subversive micropractices at the multiple sites of oppression, targeted
in multiracial, multiclass coalition work.

Perhaps the most important point to remember is that white
people are not doomed to be white supremacists. Historically, some
courageous whites have always joined multitudes of people of color
in challenging, resisting, and refusing to be overwhelmed by white
dominance. We begin to dismantle whiteness when we embark on
the long, hard struggle of basing our personal identities on political
consciousness and action, not on skin color or cultural status. Personal identity is created not by the domination of others, but by justice making in solidarity with others. As a result, *defining our political
commitments and what we do with our time and energy and money is more
important than defining our social location in determining who we are.*[77]
Hope comes also from the writings and actions of people of color
who insist that whites become good allies to them.[78]

Coalition politics is based on the moral knowledge that the system of white racial identity is constructed to diminish the relational
capacity of whites as it reinforces other systems that hurt whites. Shared
understandings of power and human need provide common ground
and a positive alternative to guilt as a primary response to white privilege. Resistance to white hegemonic power is revitalizing the labor
movement and community organizing throughout the country by
those advocating workers' rights, civil rights, and human rights.[79] Stay-
ing in coalition with others sustains the struggle for the long haul and
counteracts white people's hopelessness and impatience when social
transformation does not come quickly.

Coalition politics is not easy for whites because it requires
multicultural competence, participatory group process, and democratic
decision making—all fundamental elements of social justice that white
supremacy rejects. Coalition politics is hard for people taught to reject the erotic, playful, and creative self. Coalition politics is hard for
people taught to live in ways that are "based on injury, insult and
exclusion."[80] Coalition politics is hard for people socialized within
an anticooperative society that is saturated with the hierarchies of
business, academia, church, sports, and military training.[81]

Ethicist Elizabeth Bounds identifies a model of community in which the common good cannot be achieved apart from ongoing conflict and negotiation of difference. Here is, in my judgment, a good model of coalition work.[82] Few of us have experience with egalitarian and participatory political practices that actually welcome conflict for purposes of clarification and transformation. However, as Sharon Welch reminds us, without conflict, difference, and diversity, we lack the means for ongoing self-criticism.[83] Without conflict and negotiation, we lack exposure to the narrative of the other, to which we must deeply listen so that the white supremacist narrative within us is changed.[84]

Learning from the beloved and despised other also means challenging docility and compliance and learning how to resist. It involves embracing the gifts of blackness. These gifts, as W. E. B. DuBois identified them, include "a sensuous receptivity to the beauty of the world" and a steadfast refusal to be the "mechanical draft horse" at the service of grim powers oblivious to its beauty.[85]

Only this kind of collective engagement and democratic experimentation begins to awaken in us a passion for justice, sustains resistance to injustice, and envisions viable social alternatives.[86] Only this kind of collective engagement and democratic experimentation can dismantle white hegemonic power.

Melanie Kaye Kantrowitz, a Jew long involved in social justice work, concludes: "I may be secular but I know holiness when I hear it. One of its names is solidarity, the opposite of whiteness. The more you claim it, honor it, and fight for it, the less it costs."[87]

3

An Economic Ethics of Right Relationship

I have to struggle with my reluctance to understand how the
money that I earn is suffused with the pain and blood of people
in the past and in the present.

—Minnie Bruce Pratt

One of the worst industrial fires to date in the history of capitalism was the May 10, 1993, fire at the Kader Industrial Toy Company
in Bangkok, Thailand. The official (most likely underestimated) dead
numbered 188 persons. All but 14 were women or girls, some as young
as thirteen years of age.[1] Like the 1991 Imperial Foods fire in Hamlet,
North Carolina, cited at the beginning of chapter 1, this event was
buried in the back pages of major newspapers. As noted previously,
when workers die, especially workers who are female, young, and of
color, the world barely notices.

This chapter is devoted to an analysis of the class system, a major
structure at work in these industrial fires. While race and gender subordination also deeply structure these events, class analysis is fundamental to understanding them, including how race and gender work
in the economy and society at large. Yet class is the structure most
people in our society are the least equipped to understand.

The Taboo Social System of Class

Social theorist David Harvey contrasts the spare media coverage of the
1991 Imperial Foods fire with the media preoccupation with two other
events at the time: the sexual harassment charges against Supreme
Court nominee Clarence Thomas, and the brutal beatings of motorist
Rodney King. Harvey observes that gender and race oppression in non-
working-class contexts are not as hidden by the U.S. media as are class

politics and economic exploitation. Perhaps exploring issues of racism and sexism is less threatening to the status quo than unmasking economic and political power. However inadequate the exploration, racism and sexism can be discussed long before class issues are ever raised, especially analysis that shows how a relative few at the top of the economic system monopolize control over the labor process, the social wealth others produce, and culture and politics as well.[2]

I explore the structure of class as a way of discerning the material basis of our relationships to one another, especially the material basis of race and sex/gender relations. While many people have race and gender identities, fewer have a class identity. While class by no means exhausts the meaning of race and gender, we will not fully address racism and sexism until we help people form class identity. Two groups are fundamental to class relations, capitalists and workers. The capitalist class exercises the most power in the political economy because it owns and controls the means of producing social wealth (including land, factories, offices, machines, natural resources, human labor, stocks, and other assets). The economic power of the capitalist class means that it also controls government and cultural institutions.

The basic contradiction at the center of the capitalist system reveals itself when, in their search for unlimited profits, capitalists exhaust and destroy the very means of producing social wealth. People are worked to death, resources become extinct, and the land is irradiated. Capitalist control of culture and government means that, despite twenty-five years of environmental policies, "global warming, ozone depletion, species extinction, rain forest destruction, desertification, and the contamination of our land, water, and air by toxic chemicals, oil spills, radiation leaks, and pesticide use continue largely unabated."[3] As we shall see, capitalists not only exhaust the means of producing social wealth, they also increasingly eliminate the markets they need to sell the wealth.

The second major class in the capitalist system, the working class, has only or primarily labor to sell for a wage or a salary in order to make a living. The capitalist class, less than 10 percent of the population, makes the labor of working-class people, roughly 90 percent of the population, a commodity that capitalists buy in order to make profits for stockholders. While all working-class people share the reality that selling their productive abilities is their only or primary to sustain themselves and their families, the working class is deeply divided by income, race, and gender. Some working-class groups (less than 20 percent of workers) have some degree of control over their labor process and enjoy comfortable lifestyles because of relatively high salaries. But most in the working class (more than two-thirds of workers), often by virtue of their already subordinate status because of race and gender, have little control over their labor. They represent cheap and especially lucrative labor for capitalist profit making.

Only by exploring class relations can we see how subordinate class position unites a majority of people who are otherwise separated by attributes of difference, such as income, race, gender, and sexuality. As David Harvey suggests, this may be the main reason this culture is silent about class and yet willing (however poorly) to discuss sexism and racism. If persons with different incomes and divided by race and gender recognized their common class position in relation to capitalists, new alliances might be forged that make a claim on their fair share of social and economic power, and the class system might be transformed. Consequently, it is important to the status quo that subordinate groups remain fragmented by different social identities (as professionals or laborers, as women, people of color, gays, etc.) and people remain ignorant about class.

Working-class divisions remain strong when people believe the myth that there are three, not two, classes: upper, lower, and middle. People believe that with hard work they can leave the working class and join the superior ranks of professionals and managers, mistakenly called the middle class. So-called middle-class people are those who make higher salaries than the workers below them. They identify their interests with capitalists, even though most have only their labor to sell for a living. They are largely unaware of their common class position with workers in income brackets below them.

The task for Christians who enjoy privileges in the upper echelons of the working class, then, is to become tutored about class power. We lack power in relation to capitalists, but we benefit from the exploitation of the lower tiers of the working class. We need to understand better how we participate in some privileges of the capitalist class through our income, race, or gender, as well as how we benefit from a system that reproduces hardship, suffering, and sometimes death for the majority of workers. This is difficult work because, as economic actors, we are seldom taught to evaluate economic relationships as social power relations. Rather, we are encouraged to consume profit and pleasure as if we are isolated individuals. Moreover, even though we may presently enjoy a relatively high income and a sense of economic security, we need awareness of our increasing vulnerability as members of the working class in a radically changing economy.

Blood on Our Food, Tears on Our Clothes

This chapter explores a taboo: the reality of class. Describing the basic geography of class privilege and exploitation, I offer a brief summary of the historical evolution of the class system in the twentieth century. It is also important to make a case for understanding the history and dynamics of class as pivotal work for Christians, especially affluent ones. Since Christianity puts the neighbor in need at the center of its tradition, affluent Christians should know the forces at work that generate deteriorating conditions for the majority of the world's workers. These are the persons who lie behind the food, clothing, shelter, and other commodities and services that maintain affluent lifestyles, not only for capitalists but also for those of us in the upper tiers of the working class. Without this kind of investigation, privileged Christians suffer ignorance concerning how our lives of relative affluence and security are connected to others on whom we depend.

While we purchase symbols (Nikes not shoes, Volvos not cars), do we realize that many on whom we depend live without meeting basic human needs? The reason is the economic structure of class. A critical analysis of class, as well as resources from the Christian tradition, will help us connect the suffering of industrial fires and similar events to people like us whose salaries enable us to eat meat, wear designer clothes, and buy toys produced through that suffering.

Notions of free markets, labor contracts and money, and the language we are given to talk about the economy make it impossible to think relationally and historically about the economy. The economy itself is conventionally viewed as a natural system rather than something humanly produced and humanly transformable. We are taught that economic actors function as autonomous individuals rather than as members of groups who interact with disproportionate amounts of power. In addition, economic concepts are presented as if they are universal, unchangeable laws. Such concepts hide how we are intimately connected to the people who produce our food, clothing, housing, and all the artifacts and services we depend on daily.

In contrast to popular understanding, the economy is not just an economic regime. *More fundamentally, the economy is a system of social relations among groups of people, earth's other creatures, and the environment.* This system of social relations has developed over time and binds us intimately, though invisibly, with others. These lived connections are hidden by notions such as markets, money, and labor contracts, which only distance us from the capitalist class above and from people in the working class below. As Christians concerned with the moral quality of our relations with one another and with the earth, we need to uncover and explicitly name the social relations of class. This analysis will help us understand the nature of the bonds between ourselves and others in this economy so that we can address economic injustice and unshared cultural and political power.

To deepen understanding about class, I will first explore how Scripture and church tradition impel Christian concern about unjust class relations. Then I will briefly describe class structure before summarizing the historical evolution of class relations in late-twentieth-century global capitalism. I will then look closely into who lives, suffers, and dies behind the largely invisible structure of class. The capitalist class is making increasing profits off such lower-working-class groups as agricultural workers, sweatshop workers, prison and child laborers, and workfare recipients. However, even those of us in the upper echelons of the working class, though privileged by the class system, suffer economic vulnerability and moral damage. Finally, I offer suggestions about how to transform the structure of class.

Scripture, Tradition, and Class Power

Taking Christian tradition seriously gives ample reason for concern about class. Scripture scholar Norman Gottwald gives an account of the biblical foundations that critique class elitism. Working his way n Hebrew to Greek scriptures, Gottwald describes three major moments of community struggle by early Jews and Christians against unshared class power. The Exodus, a jailbreak engineered by the bottom class of the society, embodied the resistance of ordinary people to a tributary mode of production that enslaved them to maintain privilege for the few at the top.[4] Philosopher Michael Lerner adds that as Judaism developed, it ridiculed religious practices that lost touch with a God who enabled "ordinary people to triumph over the claims of entrenched ruling elites."[5]

Building on this tradition, Gottwald identifies a second wave of Jewish faith, embodied in the prophetic challenge to the kings of Israel who pauperized the majority by expropriation of land, debt peonage, and state taxation. While the prophetic tradition can be critiqued for its negative images of women and warriorlike images of God, its class analysis is compelling. The prophets proclaimed God's outrage at a society in which wealth and luxurious living were built on the backs of those who suffered economic misery. Though largely ignored by First World Christians, biblical tradition is clear that poverty is not a mark of having sinned, but a result of being sinned against. The ancient prophets knew that God is outraged by poverty. Not only is it unjust that some have little or nothing in the midst of plenty, but the abundance going to the rich has been gained from the deliberate exploitation and oppression of poor people.[6]

Among the thousands of verses about the poor in the Bible, Isaiah (3:13–15), Jeremiah (22:13–17), and Amos (8:4–6) provide particularly clear examples of the insight that poor people are the source of the wealth that has been stolen from them by the affluent. This claim is also present in the Jubilee tradition, or "the acceptable year of the Lord," found in Leviticus (Lev. 25:1–14). The goals of Jubilee, the same goals Jesus announces for his life and ministry at the beginning of the Gospel of Luke (Luke 4:14–21), are achieved only when what has been stolen from those at the bottom of society is returned to them. God's justice requires economic restoration.

Gottwald states that a third wave of biblical economic ethics emerged in the Jesus movement, which reaffirmed the communitarian ethics and socioeconomic practice that Christians inherited from Judaism. Early Christians embodied a discipleship of equals that in-

cluded converts drawn from diverse social classes, genders, and ra-
cial/ethnic groups.[7] Scripture scholar Marcus Borg says that *Jesus perceived wealth not as a characteristic belonging to individuals but as a product of belonging to an oppressive social class.* Jesus and the movement he
founded "subverted the world of convention and imaged an alternative way of life."[8] Gottwald adds that in nearly all periods of Jewish
and Christian history, voices have criticized economic injustice as contrary to God's creation. Active resistance requires diverse practices such
as charity, voluntary poverty, reform, and revolution.[9]

This strong predisposition toward communitarian values continues in current teachings of Christian churches. Catholic social teaching embodies a perspective on economic justice that is shared by many
Protestant denominations as well.[10] The Catholic tradition has more
than a hundred years of modern teaching about economic justice that
generally supports the class system, but with the qualifier that classes
should not become polarized. Nevertheless, this cautionary tendency
does not exhaust the Catholic legacy. Developed by popes and regional bodies of bishops since the end of the nineteenth century, this
tradition also encourages elites to be critical of the class system and
promote fundamental social change.[11]

One key legacy is Pope John Paul II's mandate "to honor the truth
that private property is under a social mortgage."[12] By this the pope
means that collective goods in society, which should be read to include the well-being of humans, creatures, and the ecosystem itself,
"constitute the essential framework for the legitimate pursuit of personal goods on the part of each individual."[13] As the pope claims, no
one can pursue individual or group goods without the support of this
larger environment, including a wide range of human, animal, and
ecological resources. Therefore, anyone pursuing individual goods
must pay back the social mortgage on what he or she has used.

In another teaching, John Paul II says the social mortgage is
what is owed by capital, or money-making interests, to labor. John
Paul identifies human work as the source of wealth because capital
is "the historical heritage of human labor." Work, not capital or
money, is the major source of the real wealth in the society. The
needs of workers have priority over the interests of employers and
stockholders. Indeed, those who own and control capital, says the

pope, are subordinate to the "right common to all to use the goods of all creation."[14]

The Canadian Catholic bishops have extended this insight about the priority of labor to include the need for "communities and working people [to] have effective control over both capital and technology." Otherwise, the bishops note, "the tendency is for them to become destructive forces in economic development."[15] The Canadian bishops support grassroots resistance to the status quo and the struggle to "acquire communal control over the necessary means of production" in order to "organize the economy to serve [the whole community's] basic needs."[16] For Latin American Catholic bishops, elites including the church can pay back on the social mortgage by practicing a "preferential option for the poor."[17] Enforcing this option does not mean asking elites to share some of their goods while maintaining the status quo. Rather, the privileged are to change sides, stand in solidarity with poor people, and resist structures and practices of exploitation and domination that benefit elites.[18]

Official Christian teaching affirms that the thrust of biblical and other theological traditions mandates Christian commitment to more inclusive economic structures than presently in place. It is also clear that this teaching remains among Christianity's best-kept secrets. Beyond "diffuse sentiment and generalized moral challenge," Gottwald says, *none* of the official churches assists people in analyzing the roots of poverty or other forms of economic injustice.[19] Knowledge about how the class structure impacts groups differently is largely unknown to First World Christians. However, knowledge about class is essential so that Christians, as moral agents, can both analyze and address how the economy promotes or obstructs the realization of biblical values and contemporary social justice principles.

Camouflaging Group Membership

In popular discourse, class is defined according to individual income or capacity to consume products and services. This notion, measuring how groups of individuals are related because they enjoy similar economic rewards such as income and prestige, is rooted in the work of sociologist Max Weber.[20] Contrary to the biblical view, which gards class as a relationship among groups, this notion perceives wealth and poverty as characteristics belonging to individuals. People who adopt this view often believe that two minorities, one very affluent and the other poor, live in a society with a middle-class majority of individuals who consume comfortably.

Even if one were to subscribe to a view of class based only on consumption capacity, this view of a comfortable middle majority could not be further from the actual incomes of U.S. households. As of 1997, 20 percent of households in the United States made $20,586 or less a year; 40 percent earned $36,000 or less. This income is not enough or hardly enough to afford a modestly affluent lifestyle for two-fifths of U.S. households. In addition, many households with incomes approximating $80,000 a year think of themselves as middle income when, in fact, they are upper income. Almost 80 percent of households bring in less than they do.[21]

This chapter defines class not primarily according to an *individual household's* income level or *consumption* capacity, but according to group membership, including the *group's relationship* to the *production* of social wealth. Class here is defined by the relations among social groups as they go about producing goods and services rather than by consumption, an idea familiar to the biblical prophets and deeply probed by Karl Marx in the nineteenth century. Class as a system of social relations based on capitalist production continues to be developed by the Marxist tradition today.[22]

If the economy is fundamentally a system of social relations, it is important to understand how the two major classes relate to each other, including what each does *for* and *to* the other. For purposes of a working definition, we might say that classes are groups of people who, because of their leisure, employment or forced unemployment, and the power they experience in relation to other groups, have a common interest in either maintaining the system or changing it.[23] While the relation of different groups to the process of production is complex and intertwined so that no paradigm can adequately reflect it, I offer the following simplified framework for defining the two major classes in U.S. society, the capitalist class and the working class. As mentioned previously, while the capitalist class is united in its control of the major economic, political, and cultural institutions of society, the working class is deeply divided, not only by income levels, but also by gender, race, and other differences.

At the top of the class structure is the capitalist class, the group that owns and controls the means of producing social wealth. The means of producing social wealth, *itself primarily the product* of the labor of the working class, includes the factories, offices, natural and human resources, and financial capital needed to produce profits, products, and services. In recent decades, the U.S. capitalist class has increased its control over social wealth. Constituting less than 10 percent of the U.S. population, this class in 1976 owned 49 percent of the wealth (all that can be personally owned, especially income-producing property). By 1995, the top 10 percent of the population controlled more than 71 percent of the wealth, including 90 percent of publicly held stocks. Since 1980, the dividends from these stocks have increased by more than 250 percent.[24]

Due in large part to corporate and upper-income tax reductions during and after the Reagan administration, wealth has become even more highly concentrated. In 1976 the top 1 percent owned 19 percent of the wealth. By 1995 they owned 47.2 percent of the wealth and 51.4 percent of all publicly held stocks.[25] *This small group of people in the top 1 percent of the nation number two to three million at most and share a greater net wealth than the bottom 95 percent combined.*[26] The entire capitalist class can live off its income-producing properties without holding jobs. Often residing in gated neighborhoods, while attending private schools and holding memberships in exclusive international clubs with other members of the world capitalist class, U.S. capitalists live in a different world from most Americans.

The capitalist class controls the economy and the major social institutions in the society. Its goal is to make the highest possible profits for shareholders (primarily themselves) from their ownership and control of factories, offices, land, raw materials, human labor, and investment capital. The capitalist class does this by strict management of various sectors of the working class and the labor process itself. The U.S. capitalist class, along with the world capitalist classes, also controls the international working class through such institutions as the CIA, the School of the Americas, the U.S. military, NATO, and global financial institutions such as the International Monetary Fund and the World Bank.

Capitalists determine which products and services are generated, how and where they are made, and how the profits from these working-class endeavors are reinvested. The capitalist class also financially supports and controls the major political and cultural institutions in the society. These are run by the upper sectors of the working class, professionals and managers, to insure that social institutions remain hospitable to the status quo. *Largely invisible to most Americans, the capitalist class decides how most people spend most of their time, what their living conditions will be, and how they will think about themselves and their relations to others.*

The other major class, the working class, is defined by its subordination to the capitalist class since working people, whatever their income level, have only their labor or primarily their labor or productive abilities to sell in order to live. The highly diversified U.S. working class includes professionals and managers occupying its upper echelons, but constituting less than 20 percent of U.S. workers. While there are different levels of managerial authority and professional status in this upper-working-class group, it includes small business owners, doctors, lawyers, academics, journalists, and some CEOs. The upper tiers of the working class also include semiprofessionals, such as schoolteachers, librarians, nurses, and lower management workers. These groups receive some privileges associated with the capitalist class, which they buy with relatively high income. But they receive higher income and status only if they produce, control, and disseminate knowledge and services supportive of the status quo. Professionals promote and maintain the existing class structure by holding positions in law, medicine, education, business, government, and the media, including television and the major journals and newspapers.[27]

On behalf of the owners of businesses and corporations, managers spend most of their time controlling the lower tiers of the working class who produce the goods and services but receive little benefit from them. Professionals and semiprofessionals are supposed to sell the capitalist system to their class while providing the educational, health care, legal, business, and entertainment services to maintain the working class as a whole. Politicians rely on taxes that come disproportionately from the working class to subsidize the military, health, insurance, oil, and other capitalist industries, which provide the money to elect them to office.

Without primary ownership of the means of production, the upper tiers of the working class mainly derive income from salaries. These salaries are often significantly higher than the wages of workers below them. Living in separate neighborhoods, with distinctive lifestyles and expensive consumption habits, the upper echelons of the working class rarely identify with workers below them. This remains the case even though most professionals and semiprofessionals, like those below them, have only or primarily their productive abilities to sell in order to make a living. However, a real difference divides workers. Although the working class does not own the means of production, many in the upper tiers of this class exercise a relative degree of control over their labor process. This control is not true for the vast majority of those in the working class.

The working class is also divided by gender. Gender divisions in the working class include the fact that in the 1990s women as a group earned between 70 and 89 percent of what men in their racial group earned. The relatively recent decrease in the gender wage gap is primarily due to falling real wages among men. However, on average, women earned one-fifth less than men in 1997.[28] As a result of this and other factors, even though women are nearly half the workforce, women's official poverty rate is about double that for men (13.7 percent compared to 6.8 percent).[29]

Class is also deeply conditioned by race. For example, the majority of professionals and semiprofessionals in the United States are white, but some African Americans have joined them in increasing numbers over the last two decades. At least one in seven African American families resides in the professional/managerial sector of the working class.[30] This is in sharp contrast to the deteriorating conditions of lower-working-class African Americans. When we look at the situation of African Americans as a whole, we find that in the early 1990s the average annual income of an African American was only 59 percent that of a white person's income, while Latino income is even less, 53 percent.[31] While the racial income gap is very wide, the racial wealth gap is even worse. Comparing household net worth, which is

the total assets of all households minus their debts, is one way
measure relative wealth. In 1995, the median black household had a
net worth of 12 percent of the median wealth for whites ($7,400 com-
pared to $61,000) and the median Hispanic household had a net worth
of only 8 percent of the median wealth for whites ($5,000 compared
to $61,000).[32]

However, the working class is more deeply divided by income than
it is by gender and race. Differences in earnings between men and
women and between whites and communities of color, while significant, are not as great as differences in income between the upper and
lower sectors of the working class. As Michael Zweig points out, while
men working full-time earned 1.4 times as much as women working
full-time in 1986, and while whites working full-time earned 1.3 times
as much as blacks, managers and professionals made 2.3 times the
income of service workers.[33] Since this time the differentials between
professionals and service workers have only increased. Between 1989
and 1997, wages were flat or falling for the bottom 80 percent of
workers. Only professionals in the upper 20 percent of the wage scale
obtained real wage growth from 1989 to 1997.[34] People are poor or
rich in this country primarily because of their location in the class
system. That is the basic truth, even though the class structure uses
racism and sexism to justify the deep divisions in working-class income. Racism and sexism give a "commonsense" explanation for the
stratification within the working class and hide the enormous polarization between the working class as a whole and the capitalist class.

Dividing the Working Class by Income

In recent decades, due to major shifts in the U.S. economy, many professionals and managers have seen their positions erode, in terms of
losing control over their work, their salaries stagnating or declining,
or their positions disappearing altogether.[35] Many in the upper working class are experiencing increased powerlessness and economic vulnerability. Similar to low-paid workers, professionals and managers
not subject to downsizing often keep their jobs at the price of overwork.[36] Increasingly, they manage large coteries of part-time and con-

tingent workers while also doing clerical functions inherited from the decline in secretarial and other support staff.[37]

Because most people in the upper tiers of the working class identify with the capitalist class and not with other workers, they are often surprised when their education, their maleness, or their whiteness no longer protects them from the vulnerability familiar to the rest of the working class. Educator Carmen Vasquez observes that the so-called middle-class camouflage of working-class chemists, teachers, and managers is revealed, however, when they lose their paychecks and move closer to inhabiting the same rung on the class ladder as the hamburger flipper who has been there her whole life. Vasquez calls on all who do not control production to recognize and defend one another.[38]

Others in the upper working class are doing exceptionally well. They have seen salaries, benefits, and other perks significantly increase in the past two decades. This is particularly true of those in the real-wage growth sector of high-technology jobs, including computers, software, communication, and information technologies. These technologies are not only driving the economy, but also de-skilling working-class labor and increasing centralized control over the work site for all workers.[39] Members of the professional/managerial working class who own a disproportionate share of the 10 percent of publicly held stock (stock held apart from pensions) not controlled by the capitalist class often wish to grow their assets so that they can become owners of the means of production and join the capitalist class. In addition, their attitudes toward the lower members of their class are no different from those of capitalists: workers should provide labor at the lowest possible cost.

It is difficult to provide precise estimates of where the upper working class resides within existing income statistics because income does not always reflect actual class position. However, if we divide U.S. individual and family income into quintiles, the less than 20 percent of U.S. workers who are professionals and semiprofessionals most likely fall in the lower echelons of the top quintile of workers whose households brought in over $80,000. They are especially concentrated in the upper echelons of the second quintile whose households in 1997 earned between $53,616 and $80,000.[40]

The third and largest sector of the U.S. class system, more than two-thirds of the total labor force, is the lower tiers of the working class, including clerical workers, skilled manual workers, and workers who are unskilled or have been de-skilled. The economic status of this sector is deteriorating rapidly. Economist Zweig describes the lower working class as including "those who are employed by others, do not supervise others, and have little autonomy over their work."[41] A few may own stock, but it affords them no control over capitalists or their own labor process. Their role is to work for wages, and their wages constitute significantly less wealth than they have actually created so as to produce capitalist profits. They also are the clientele for the upper working class who charge them high prices for professional services. However, professionals expect services provided by the lower working class to remain plentiful and inexpensive.

The lower sectors of the working class are found in the lower echelons of the second quintile of workers making between $53,616 and $80,000 and among the 60 percent of U.S. households with incomes in 1997 in the bottom three quintiles. They include the 20 percent, respectively, which brought in between $53,616 and $36,000 and between $36,000 and $20,586 as well as those in the bottom 20 percent, which brought in $20,586 or less.[42]

Given these statistics, it is evident that the lower tiers of the working class contain increasingly impoverished workers. Even though the official poverty line for a family of four in 1998 was $16,700, consider the studies that show the very minimum it takes for families to be economically self-sufficient. For example, studies for the State of Massachusetts found that a typical family of one adult and two children (one preschooler, one school-age child) in the central part of the state in 1997 must have earned approximately $35,460 a year, or $2,955 a month, or $16.79 an hour, to survive without government subsidies. Self-sufficiency is based on the simplest possible lifestyle that a working family could adopt without having to make trade-offs in necessities, such as cutting out food for heat or forgoing health care for child care.[43]

The lower sectors of the working class, the vast majority of U.S. workers, are always trading off on necessities given the ubiquity of low-wage work in a high-cost economy. These sectors include the 28.6

percent of U.S. workers who held full-time jobs in 1997 that did not pay them enough to live even above the official poverty level, calculated at a rate far below the self-sufficiency standard.[44] They include the almost two-thirds of U.S. workers who do not have wholly employer-financed medical insurance.[45] Millions of these workers make ends meet only through overtime, or as multiearner families with each partner having multiple jobs.[46]

Due to changes in the global economy, the real wages for the bottom 60 percent of workers have declined between 12 and 18 percent from 1979 to 1997.[47] With low-wage industries accounting for 79 percent of all new jobs, vast numbers of young lower-working-class whites and people of color are being condemned to minimum-wage, low-skill, and no-benefit work.[48] Beneath them are increasing numbers who cannot find work or can find only part-time, contingent work. Companies decrease costs by hiring people during peak periods or periods of expanding output, only to fire them when production slows down.

Moreover, the professional/managerial sector is designing computers that further de-skill work so that more work can be downsized and outsourced. Historically, this follows the logic of the capitalist class, which has always sought to control and divide workers and devalue work by de-skilling craftspersons and creating the fragmented assembly-line worker. This historical process has now accelerated to include not only manual work in automated factories but also mental work in automated offices.[49] In tandem with the clericalization of professional workers, we see the professionalization of some sectors of the lower working class. For example, like professionals, more and more people doing clerical work and other forms of administrative support are expected to learn increasing numbers of skills on their own time while their salaries remain the same or erode.[50]

As a result of this kind of technological "progress," one-third of U.S. workers are contingent workers, who work from day to day, week to week, or month to month. Economist Juliet Shor says that in the past two decades, those working part-time but desiring full-time work have increased more than seven times. She observes that "the US economy is increasingly unable to provide work for its population," certainly work that will lift people above poverty.[51] Meanwhile, as adults lack work, the International Labor Organization estimated in 1998 that between 200 and 400 million children are working worldwide in economic activities apart from domestic services in households. These include millions of children five to fourteen years old who work in agriculture, factories, and the service sector.[52] They include not only children in forced child labor camps in places such as China and Burma but an estimated 290,000 minors in the United States who are illegally employed at some point during a given year. These children, often doing hazardous work, earn on average $1.38 per hour less than legal young adults. Despite the lack of reliable employment data on children, it is estimated that U.S. children's labor adds up to a cost saving of $155 million per year for businesses. With increasing poverty in the United States and elsewhere, child labor will no doubt grow steadily in the future.[53] This radical restructuring of the labor market to meet the profit-making needs of the capitalist class helps explain the deep divisions between the upper and lower sectors of the working class. It explains why the average income of the top 20 percent is nine times that of the lowest 20 percent. The gap between upper-income and lower-income families in the United States is the widest since the Census Bureau began collecting the data in 1947.[54]

At the very bottom of the working class are adults who work for subminimum wages, such as workfare recipients and the 10 percent of prison laborers who now make profits for capitalists.[55] The bottom of the working class also includes unemployed impoverished people who serve the upper class as reserve labor, keeping wages down when they do not have work and standing ready to be absorbed when the economy needs more workers. These people are often forced to subsist on crime, in the underground economy, and on rapidly eroding state welfare programs. Americans living below the official poverty line number nearly 36 million people, half of whom are white.[56]

When we see how the lower working class provides superexploitable labor and other functions (such as suffering unemployment to keep the general wage level down) that are essential to maintain profits for the capitalist class, it is difficult to believe the dominant ideology asserting that education is the answer to upward mobility for the lower working class. If everyone in the lower working class became educated and moved to the upper tiers of the working class, who would do the worst work in the society for the lowest wages? Who would provide the basis for the affluent lifestyles of the upper working class and the capitalist class? Only relatively few token persons are allowed to leave the lower working class. When a few move up, they do not offer significant competition for professional managerial jobs. They also help maintain the ideology of hard work and the unquestioned privileges of those above.

Dividing the Working Class by Race and Gender

Political theorist David Harvey maintains that class is the material site where multiple forms of oppression coalesce.[57] He also contends that we must work to address the injustice of class power without using class to marginalize other unjust power relations.[58] We can appreciate, for example, that disproportionate numbers of people of color and white women occupy the sectors of the lower working class because people's subordinate status in the gender and race hierarchies renders them easy targets for superexploitation in the economy. If all workers are essential to support profit making and are subject to receiving less than they produce by the capitalist class, then race and gender subordination further isolate those who must specialize in doing the worst work for the least amount.

Race and gender subordination are useful to justify the poverty or lower-working-class status of people without having to analyze the class system itself. The dynamics of class remain invisible by burying the issue of monopolized class power under questions of gender and race. When people are able to blame poverty on supposedly inferior races and supposedly weaker, less-competent females, they are less likely to notice the class structure itself. Yet much (though certainly not all) of the pain of race and gender oppression is rooted in the class structure, which exploits these and other oppressions so thoroughly. When people struggle against class, they are really working against the material basis of all subordination. Since this is the case, we need to pursue economic justice in order to redress injustices of racism and sexism and also to seek justice for white working-class men.

The Ideology of Hard Work and Bad Luck

While class is invisible as a meaningful social category in the United States, it conditions our lives in the most fundamental ways. Class has life-shaping consequences in terms of our personal sense of entitlement (or lack thereof), our degree of access to the social, political, and economic benefits of the society, and our likelihood of having to do the worst and most dangerous jobs in the society. Class is essential to the construction of our identities as capitalist people, the interpretation of our experiences, and the things we learn to desire. Class is encoded into our speech, dress, and assumptions about ourselves and others. Socialization into the class system is done through multiple institutions, including the family, the state, education, and the media. If we are to take moral and personal responsibility for our lives, we must become self-aware about how our class position has taught us to think about the world and our place in it.

To maintain the class system, elites especially are socialized into an "I versus others" worldview that supports individualism and self-interest at the expense of others. This worldview would have us believe that the relations people have with one another through the market are socially just. It would have us believe that the monopolization of control over the economy by the wealthy should be celebrated as "democracy," "freedom," and "human rights."[59] It would have us believe that the benefits bestowed on us, the upper echelons of the working class who think of ourselves as the middle class, are what we have received according to our individual merit. It would have professionals and managers believe that it is only right and just that lower-working-class people support our lifestyles with low-cost production and services. Perhaps most important, it would have professionals and managers believe that they are fundamentally distinct from the lower working class and have no commonality with them vis-à-vis a relationship to the capitalist class characterized by exploitation.

We learn that capitalist leaders know what is best for us, that they use science and technology to enhance our lives, and that under their tutelage we will have access to more and better jobs if we are prepared for them. And if we are not prepared for the future, we have only ourselves to blame. In order that we will not notice the enormous stratification in income and access to resources, we learn that we have a unified society with a level playing field in which most people are flourishing under social cooperation. This is generally true for everyone except inferior races and genders and other individuals who do not work hard enough or are subject to random bad luck. Professionals, semiprofessionals, and those preparing to enter their ranks learn that we have nothing in common with those who are not doing well in the economy. We think of them as relatively few since we believe that most people have access to the privileges and resources we do.

Thus, it becomes easy to justify our positions and the unearned privileges we enjoy, as well as the suffering of the lazy or unlucky "less fortunate" others. We learn that self-discipline and hard work usually pay off, and due to our own hard work and individual merit, we are entitled to things that other people do not have. Socialization into the class structure gives us permission to be good capitalist people, dedicated to pursuing private consumption and profits and living without accountability to others, especially without obligations to share with them. Indeed, we learn mostly to admire and identify with those above us in the class system and to blame those below us. In this way, the ideology protecting our privileges in the upper tiers of the working class conditions us to deny attention and feeling to those we have learned are unworthy. To maintain unearned entitlement for some, the professional/managerial sector must be carefully taught to deny not only the privileges of so-called middle-class background, education, and other unearned resources, but also our common class position with those below us, including their suffering and the claims they make on us.[60]

Critically examining how we have been tutored in the social relations of class helps us see that *class is not a property of individuals and individual merit, but a way that groups consolidate social, political, and economic power.* Contrary to what we are told, most privilege is not earned, and most poverty is not deserved. Poverty is not the lot of "unfortunate" people suffering from random bad luck, for "the poor do not cause their own poverty any more than the wealthy create their own wealth."[61] People largely get their poverty or their wealth depending on their location in the class system.

Being tutored in the social relations of class power also helps us see that many of the increasing problems in the upper working class, such as downsizing, wage stagnation, and overwork, are rooted in the capitalist class rather than in those unemployed or underemployed in the lower working class. For most people with privilege, possessions and status have been won on the shoulders of the lower working class. They provide the available goods and services but, except for a token few, are barred from competing with the professional/managerial sector at the higher levels of the capitalist race. In making moral evaluations about our relations to others, Christians should be speaking about class power, how we participate in it, how we benefit from it, who lacks it, and how we share common vulnerability with those below us. As Christian ethicist Beverly Harrison says, proper theological work involves exposing the dynamics, including the class dynamics, that prevent just relationship among human communities.[62]

To continue this theological work of unmasking how we benefit from aspects of class power even as we are excluded from it, we need to move beyond the U.S. class framework to consider class relations in an increasingly globalized economy. To deepen an ethical evaluation of class relations, we need to understand not only the basic structure of class, but also how class relations have evolved in late-twentieth-century global corporate capitalism. Class dynamics are changing due to the increasing globalization of capitalism as it becomes a fully integrated world system.

Controlling Class Relations through Competition

Given the structure of class elucidated here, it is apparent that social relations under capitalism cannot accommodate accountability between groups or equitable relations among people. As I have argued, if the most powerful 10 percent in U.S. society owns and controls capital (including human labor) in order to make the highest possible profits for investors, then the following must happen for the system to work: the professional/managerial sector must indoctrinate everyone into the basic goodness and "efficiency" of the capitalist project; the lower working class must be pressured to accept the lowest possible wages with the harshest conditions and lowest pay going to the weakest members of society; and the earth and its resources must be available for the exploitation necessary for profit making. Minimal standards of human decency and the sustainability of the ecosystem are irrelevant to this process. Political analyst William Greider argues that everyone's sense of virtue is degraded by the present reality even though, according to the conscience of capitalism and its supposedly inevitable economic laws, there is no crime.[63] The lack of moral accountability in the class system becomes even more apparent when we examine social relations under current capitalist conditions and how they have evolved in recent history.

The profit-making role of the capitalist class necessitates making the greatest amount of product with the least possible input or cost whether from capital, labor, or raw materials. But making goods and services as cheaply as possible is only half of it. The capitalist class also needs buyers, for it needs to match supply with demand in order to maintain profit levels. Since local markets may quickly dry up, especially if potential customers make low wages as workers, capitalists always need access to new markets. New markets are essential to absorb excess product supply and to provide opportunities to reinvest the profits so that even more profit can be made.

Today the capitalist class, which possesses the technology to make business geographically mobile and highly mechanized, has access not only to a nearly inexhaustible global supply of poor people willing to work for the lowest wages, but also to mechanized labor, which can exponentially reduce cost and increase output. Consequently, the key problem of the global economy is a growing surplus of goods, labor, and productive capacity. The current ability of the capitalist classes, including the U.S. capitalist class as well as those of Europe and Asia, to increase supply intensifies the potential for oversupply and increases global competition. Competition from other firms increases the pressure on the capitalists to cut costs, including further exploiting (getting more out of us for even less) the entire working class and destroying the ecosystem.[64] But as we can see, the very remedy to the supply problem at the micro level (cut costs including wages to be more competitive with your supply) increases the problem of oversupply at the macro level as firms both increase their supplies and further impoverish working populations so as to diminish the number of people able to become their customers.

The professional/managerial sector, ever vigilant for capitalists, tells us not to worry; oversupplied markets will eventually shrink to match demand since the economy is basically self-regulating. Individual capitalists, however, keep shooting themselves in the foot, so to speak, as they exhaust both natural resources, essential to the means of producing wealth, and the buying power of workers, essential to maintain markets. Capitalists keep cutting costs that deepen the impoverishment of the working class and ecological destruction. Capitalists also do all they can in the meantime to get around these problems by designing ineffective environmental laws and increasing their access to world markets (through free trade agreements, military intervention in other countries, and neoliberal economic policies).

The historical record demonstrates the various ways the capitalist class has dealt with the problem of oversupply. In the United States, the Great Depression of 1929 was a major illustration of the illusion that a situation of excess supply and inadequate demand would self-regulate. As Greider points out, stock prices were driven up right before the crash because investors assumed erroneously that all those new factories being built could sell the things they were producing.[65] After years of suffering for the working class, especially its lower sectors, World War II ended the depression as factories worked at capacity to supply materials for war, virtually creating full employment.

After the war, the oversupply that generated the Great Depression (with too many goods chasing too few buyers) was addressed by strengthening demand through economic policy promoted by the economist John Maynard Keynes. When the government adopted Keynesian policy, the capitalist class forced itself to do what it needed to do in order to survive—accept the growth of unions and union-wage jobs and the role of the state in promoting demand and stabilizing the economy. This included vastly increased military spending (ostensibly fueled by the Cold War) to guarantee profitable military contracts for the largest corporations, government regulation of banking and monopolies, and implementation of labor laws to keep wages up. Keynesian economics also included the policies of the welfare state (including social security, unemployment insurance, food stamps), which put money into the hands of consumers.

In the 1970s, increased competition for U.S. business, due to the revival of European and Japanese capitalist classes from their weakened positions after World War II, meant an exponential growth in excess capacity. Given the new technological powers of capital to become mobile, global, and mechanized, the U.S. capitalist class has no longer been willing to support the U.S. working class by accepting unions and other policies of the welfare state of the previous era. David Loy notes that "the economic support system [including union-wage jobs and a state welfare system that was created in the 1930s] to correct the failures of capitalism is now blamed for the failures of capitalism."[66] To make this assessment stick, the capitalist class became superorganized during the 1970s and used its class power to defeat such measures as labor law reform, progressive taxes, consumer protection laws, and antitrust legislation.[67]

Since the 1980s, most of the rest of the 1930s legislation has been dismantled, including the welfare state, as the capitalist class maintains a tight grip on both major political parties. The only part of Keynesian economic policy that is in full swing is military spending, part of the New Deal legislation supporting demand that creates astronomical profits for the largest corporations. Current military spending is about $280 billion, which is 86 percent of the average ($325 billion) spent per year during the Cold War. The military budget for fiscal year 2000 is almost $290 billion, while all other domestic spending, including such worthwhile programs as education, job training, housing, medical research, environmental protection, and Head Start, will total $246 billion.[68]

In addition, the United States is the world's leading weapons dealer and is promoting militarism by zealously expanding weapons exports.[69] War benefits the current system, not only because it absorbs military products, but also because IMF and World Bank loans for rebuilding after war-making puts nations and their economies securely under the control of Western capital.[70]

As a result of increased capitalist power, the institutions of the lower working class have been greatly weakened. U.S. workers are no longer afforded a protected niche, including union-wage jobs, within the global working class. Robert Brusca, chief economist of Nikko Securities and spokesperson for the managerial sector, says, "US workers will have to realize that they are now competing for jobs against people who ride to work every day on bicycles, own only one pair of shabby sandals and are prepared to live with their families crammed into tiny apartments."[71]

Obviously, an impoverished U.S. working class will not be able to consume enough to keep profits up for U.S. capitalists. Consequently, the most recent way of dealing with oversupply is not limited to cutting costs by a wage race-to-the-bottom and the mechanization of work. Perhaps even more important, dealing with oversupply includes the proliferation of "free trade agreements" that will give U.S.-based corporations, whose domestic markets are weakening, better access to global markets. The upper class now requires the state to promote not Keynesian policies to increase domestic demand, but what is called neoliberal economic policy, which claims that when governments limit access to global markets, they constrain growth, limit prosperity, and increase unemployment.

A new way of dealing with the problem of oversupply lies at the core of the capitalist system: promotion of such neoliberal economic policies as global export-oriented, highly diversified, and quick-turnover production (since mass markets are drying up, keep supplying the affluent with small batches of ever changing products); flexible labor markets (cut wages with no long-term commitment to the upper and lower tiers of the working class); fewer social services, so a country can pay back loans to rich lenders; and less environmental regulation, which cuts into profits.[72] Neoliberal policies are being implemented globally through governments that must comply with capitalist lending institutions such as the World Bank and the International Monetary Fund.

It seems clear, however, that this geographical "fix" by the capitalist classes is limited by the size of the planet, which only increases the desperate edge to global competition. Each transnational corporation (TNC) hopes that surplus supply will be resolved "when the other guy closes his factory."[73] Every corporation counts on finding a niche to protect it from the larger capitalist system. Strategies for corporate survival are variations on get-rich-quick-and-run schemes. They include forming corporate alliances to divide up the global market, exerting short-term demands for profit through diversified quick-turnover forms of production, shifting production to many markets in many regions (they cannot all fail at once), engaging in casinolike speculation in buying and selling assets through takeovers and mergers, and instituting neoliberal government policies that dismantle the welfare state and redistribute wealth in favor of the rich. And when these are not sufficient, military intervention to prevent alternative experiments keeps regions hostage to capitalist profit-making

Because 85 percent of world production is still handled by domestic corporations in a single geographic location, scholars debate the extent of globalization.[74] Currently, 15 percent of world industrial production is done by TNCs, and a significant amount of their profits comes from foreign investments. Disputing the extent of global trade, however, is not as important as recognizing a fundamental change in capitalist class power as a result of these new conditions of production. Part of this change is based on the exponential increase in the mobility of capital. Francis Piven and Richard Cloward point out that the entire working class has been weakened by the ability (whether used or not) of the capitalist class "to launch new and terrifying exit threats—by hiring contingent workers and strike replacements, by restructuring production, or by threatening to close plants or shift production elsewhere."[75]

Intensified Managerial Control

As capitalism creates increasingly segmented and authoritarian work through union busting, lower wages, de-skilling, and the threat of exit, it becomes evident that the capitalist class is as interested in control as it is in profit making. The capitalist work process is characterized by hierarchy and the use of technology to de-skill and control people. In the design of the workplace, value is placed on a few elites who dictate goals and the means to get there ("efficiency"), many goods that are delivered quickly regardless of quality ("calculability"), products and services—and people—that are scripted similarly ("predictability"), and bureaucracies that decide what people need and who gets access to information, and utilize continuously innovative technology to control workers ("control").[76] *As the capitalist class implements "flexible accumulation" and shifts work from one region of the world to another and from one product line to another while employing continuously changing technology, it functions as a permanently disruptive force.*

This process has traditionally created massive insecurity and instability for the lower working class. Once largely protected from these dynamics, the professional/managerial sector is now vulnerable to them as well.[77] Indeed, the front office and the back offices have suffered as enterprise moves industrial jobs to regions of the world without a tradition of industrial organizing, mechanizes work, or revives patriarchal subcontracting and family labor systems (sweatshops) in the United States. With the collapse of the material conditions for working-class politics, such as business dependence on a region's workforce, capitalists feel less pressure to make concessions to popular social needs.[78] At the same time that the state gives a freer hand to industry through deregulation, the structure of the global financial system is becoming more centralized. David Harvey concludes, "What is most interesting . . . is the way in which capitalism is becoming ever more tightly organized through dispersal, geographic mobility and flexible responses."[79]

Ironically, these innovative, disruptive work processes create a bland and homogenized society. One can jet travel for hours and still be in the same boring commercial landscapes, monolithic urban areas, and predictable suburbs. One can search the mainstream media in vain for variety in political perspectives. *Perhaps even more to our peril, the homogenizing of capitalist culture is built on the homogenizing of nature.* As the economic system destroys diversity in human societies, so also it destroys diversity in the ecosphere. "As hundreds of species life disappear each year and at an accelerating rate," Ynestra King argues that "nonhuman nature is being rapidly simplified, undoing the work of organic evolution."[80]

Capitalist work creates a society that emphasizes quantity with a corresponding lack of interest in quality or real variety. What is supposedly best is more of the same (whatever superficial camouflage tries to convince us otherwise) delivered quickly. This is as true of McDonald's and Pizza Hut as it is of the Internet. Native talent is replaced by machines, and people adopt corporate-designed scripts for personal emotional expression. Work and the pace of life are subject to speed up in order to shorten product turnover time and increase profits.[81] While the capitalist class struggles to win a game in which some must lose, work is grim.

Not valued in work or society are democracy, variety, continuity, production of a quality item, environmental well-being, emotional labor, including caring for children and helping people, and enjoyment of a good time.[82] In capitalist work people remain isolated, anxious, and insecure, feeling extraordinarily vulnerable to the universalizing power of the economy over their lives. One must search hard for a piece of life that is not up for sale as more areas get pulled into the profit-making system, from vacation packages to dating services to exercise clubs. Harvey maintains that the accelerating turnover in goods and services provides the material base for the accelerating turnover in values. Notions of accountability, responsibility, and commitment seem almost quaint. We have flexible, disposable workers, products, and values, as well as a master narrative shaped around the individual pursuit of an isolated self-interest.[83]

Feelings of insecurity and a lack of alternative values condition people to self-police, a dynamic fundamental to the maintenance of the class system. *However much bureaucracy and technology can control us, capitalist profits are absolutely dependent on self-disciplined workers who have internalized capitalist values and the corporate worldview.*[84] Without alternative values, good capitalist people cope with their insecurity by escaping into consumerism and the "shop till you drop" ethos, fueled by the $147 billion spent in advertising in the mid-1990s. Our desires are as socially constructed and manufactured as the goods that satisfy them.[85]

The need to manage and control is so essential to the capitalist ethos that it increasingly takes on a life of its own. The capitalist search for security in a basically insecure system means that managerial domination supersedes classical market forces. When the technology is available, *business is coordinated by manager manipulations more than by market mechanisms.* For example, Stanley Deetz observes that the coordinated capacity of managers using sophisticated telecommunications far exceeds the market in business transactions. Deetz notes that

"companies such as General Electric primarily escape classical ma[r]
forces by quickly entering and exiting different markets," according to
the get-rich-quick-and-run strategy of contemporary capitalism.[86] Deetz
claims that with nearly all fundamental economic decision making
in the hands of managers whose boards consist of managers of other
corporations, "the pursuit of profit often becomes subordinated to
the attainment of efficiency in bureaucratic organization."[87] Capitalism is evolving into a system that seeks control first and profits second. Like the student who seeks grades with learning as a by-product,
capitalism seeks control with profits as a by-product.[88] Ethicist Beverly
Harrison agrees when she recognizes the laissez-faire market of neoclassical economics as the "deism of modernity." Harrison says that
the "free market" has never existed since "the whole point of capitalism is to *control* markets."[89]

Drawing upon psychoanalytic descriptions of the "Authoritarian
Personality," Marc Estrin argues that the weak egos and sexually
repressed personalities of many corporate and political bureaucrats
drive them to a "rage for order" in which fear of social chaos, including unpredictable sexuality, may be more important than the need
to maximize profits or save money.[90] Spending on the poor, who are
often stigmatized for their sexual practices, is a particularly good
example where authoritarianism is promoted despite financial loss.
Women who have received welfare note that as government dismantles the welfare state, it is evident that the logic of spending
money on poor infants and children in order to avoid much bigger
health, education, and prison costs down the road is lost on those
who need to control and punish poor single mothers.[91] Similarly,
political theorist Carole Pateman states that capitalist owners will
not fully automate the work process, however much it reduces their
cost, because employers cannot exercise managerial control over
machines.[92]

When it becomes clear that the need to control is even stronger
than the need to cut costs, it seems that what is going on in our collective situation is more than desire for profits benefiting the top group.
To characterize such corporate and political leaders as simply greedy or
mean-spirited misunderstands the origins of managerialism in the
authoritarian personality and limits effective response.[93] Managerialism

as a set of routine practices seeks control over workers, nature, and all subordinate populations associated with nature, even at the expense of profit. The managerial impulse of the authoritarian personality will remain a critical issue for society even if the economy is democratized. The violence involved in controlling and manipulating others has always been essential to a polarized class structure. However, this violence from above is increasing in intensity as economic vulnerability climbs up the class ladder. Our social ideology, however, warns us against violence from below and only further mystifies our economic and other social relations.

Who Benefits and Who Suffers?

Who lives and suffers behind the money and goods amassed and enjoyed by elites in the system of managerial corporate capitalism? The question for an ethical economics is this: If people and the earth give of themselves to sustain me, do I have moral obligations to them? When we consume something or when we count our money, do we know what went into making the money we have or what went into making what we consume? Do we know what was destroyed, or if the workers or the ecosystem itself was justly compensated for it? In Catholic social teaching's terms, was the social mortgage paid? What do we need to know in order to develop an economic ethics of right relationship? These questions are crucial to moral agency but are not allowed to surface in capitalist culture.

Since the rise of industrialism in the eighteenth century, capitalism has meant lack of scarcity and increasing ease of life for relatively few on the planet while it chains greater numbers to brutal forms of domination. This economic system erodes moral accountability until people become organized to make it so, as they have during certain periods. The long, hard struggles for labor, civil, and women's rights are part of the history of protest of the profit-making system. People who gave their lives in these struggles are part of the enormous costs of prosperity. They are often little known or forgotten because elites do not wish to acknowledge that the basis of "the good life" is built on the abuse of others. In the early 1990s the top fifth of the world's population enjoyed 82.7 percent of total world income and consumed 66 percent of the planet's resources. This meant that two children in a superconsuming family were the equivalent of thirty to forty consumers in poor families.[94] By 1997 the share of income for the poorest fifth of the world's population had decreased from 1.4 percent of world income in 1991 to a miserable 1.1 percent. This means that the above statistics are even more highly skewed at the beginning of the twenty-first century than they were a decade ago. *This also means that the people generating the majority of food, products, services, and other resources consumed by the few are disproportionately located in the 80 percent of world population who divide up less than a third of its resources and share less than 17.3 percent of total world income.*[95]

Through the market system, these relationships remain invisible. Elites are fed, clothed, and entertained by children, women, and men whose situation as producers of the good life for us is all too often little better than slavery. The following examples uncover only the tip of the iceberg of how this is so. For a start, capitalists can contract work to thousands of small sweatshops throughout the globe that distance the owners as well as the consumers from the women, children, and men whose labor provides the base of the profit-making system. They include, for example, the twenty-five thousand mostly women and girls in Indonesia who make Nike, Reebok, Adidas, and other famous-brand shoes while living in bamboo huts and sharing a tiny living space with five or six other workers. They include the millions of Chinese who labor long hours for little pay to make the toys, leather, shirts, television sets, and other goods whose low prices benefit American consumers and whose wildcat strikes rose dramatically in the 1990s.[96] They include the millions of women, female adolescents, and children who provide sexual service stations for affluent men in Manila, Bangkok, Rio de Janeiro, and Brussels.[97]

Closer to home, they include the people who pick our tomatoes in Immokalee, Florida, for steadily declining wages over the past two decades. People who pick tomatoes make $9,000 a year with no benefits. Workers at the bottom also include California strawberry pickers who endure intense back pain, sleep on dirt floors, and make $5,000 laboring seven to nine months a year without benefits.[98] They include Mexican, Central American, and Laotian immigrants who, as mentioned in the previous chapter, cut and pack meat for low pay in the Midwest. These immigrants endure grueling work that can often be sustained for only a year or less. The Immigration and Naturalization Service, working in conjunction with taxpayer-subsidized meatpacking giants, initially looks the other way, but then deports these workers before the industry has to start paying health insurance. Thus, the government supports the capitalist class to keep labor transitory and invisible so that industry is assured an inexhaustible supply of low-wage workers.[99]

As we in the upper echelons of the working class feed, clothe, and entertain ourselves, we are intimately connected to the lives of the women, children, and men who are superexploited by terrible conditions of overwork, underpayment, deplorable living environments, and sometimes death in order to provide what we consume and what we have been taught to desire. The blood, sweat, tears, and suffering behind what we consume are carefully hidden from us. We are told instead that CEOs, mutual fund managers, investment speculators, and other members of the business hierarchy are the economic heroes who create the wealth and are benefactors of the general welfare. We are told that foreign workers get low wages because of their low productivity and that they prefer low pay to the company's pulling out. Never mind the centuries of colonial and neocolonial impoverishment by the West, which robbed them of control over their land, labor, and resources. Never mind the escalating wildcat strikes by these "contented" workers. Never mind that so much labor is done under U.S.-sponsored dictatorships notorious for human rights abuses and sustained by bloated military budgets. In the United States, we are told that low-wage workers are independent, responsible achievers, no matter how impoverished they are.

Popular ideology promulgated from academia and the media tells the rest of the working class that when we pay what the market will bear, we pay a just price for our goods. Never mind that the market bears not only unjust social relations, but the vast destruction wrought to other resources, animals, and the earth itself. Most of what we buy seems rootless and pristine. It comes in antiseptic containers, often neatly shrink-wrapped, from which all traces of connection to human, animal, and plant life, all traces of human suffering and oppressive social relations, have been expunged.[100] We are distanced from the environmental destruction and social labor that went into the goods. Resources used for the product may become extinct, or pollution from its manufacture may be more than the ecosystem can absorb. Whole human beings, often adolescents and children, are reduced to hired hands, and their blood, sweat, and tears along with the earth and its creatures are treated as if a storehouse to be plundered for our consumption. The upper working class buys in charming boutiques, designer malls, and overstuffed supermarkets in which the macabre nature of the commercial project is thoroughly masked and the origin of capitalist goods is never questioned. Like the Nazi selling of Jewish children's clothing, only the condition of the goods counts—not too many bullet holes or bloodstains.[101]

In addition, the macabre nature of capitalist commercialism is rising up to threaten more and more of us physically as well as morally. Under conditions of deepening poverty, bacteria are evolving into more virulent forms. We have seen the reemergence of diseases long thought banished, such as leprosy and tuberculosis. The majority of people with AIDS, both in the United States and in the rest of the world, are people for whom poverty is the primary and determining condition of their lives.[102]

Poverty and the system of profit making also lies at the root of the increasing contamination of the world's food supply. Here especially, the capitalist class and the working class are becoming equally susceptible. The globalization of the food system means that it is increasingly difficult to safeguard what anyone eats. U.S. supermarkets contain raw fruit, vegetables, meat, and eggs that have been saturated with pesticides banned in the United States (but sold for profits elsewhere) and/or laden with increasingly virulent food-borne infection not typically (but increasingly) found in the United States. Elites who refuse to eat fresh produce in Two-Thirds World countries return home and buy it in their local supermarkets. In addition, privileged Americans spend half their food dollar in restaurants where food-service workers, among the lowest paid in the labor market, have no health insurance, may have infectious diseases, and may not wash their hands.[103] The food system connects us all intimately, including directly exposing elites to some of the harmful effects of poverty. The contamination of the world's food system is a sobering example of how the chickens have come home to roost.

If the origin of capitalist goods is not questioned or monitored in the global economic system, neither is the origin of our money. Like market exchange, money draws a veil over the social relationships that provide the context for our money. When we analyze the historical geography of our money, for example, or our family's money, we see how it has been amassed on the backs of other groups, especially groups who suffer multiple oppressions. Minnie Bruce Pratt, a white university professor, says she cannot evaluate the money she earns without acknowledging that her family's class position, essential background for her ability to receive a Ph.D., was built on "the pain and blood of people in the past and the present." This includes a great-grandfather who took land from Creek Indians and farmed it with slave labor, a grandfather who worked as a security guard for a coal company's plunder, and a mother whose earnings came from teaching in a segregated white school while leaving her daughter, Minnie, in the care of a black woman who was paid low wages.[104]

Like Pratt, I experience the difficulty of finding out about my family's economic history. It is a history that, as Pratt says, is "hidden with a veneer of respectability and has to be pieced together through bits of conversation and my own knowledge of class theory." Most of us know more about the pedigree of our animals than of our own family class histories. The history of my "grimly held class position" includes Dutch tobacco farmers in North Carolina who made their profits off slave labor and the labor of their Cherokee wives. These native women, like my great-great-grandmother, lost their ancestral homes, were reduced to their wifely roles, and were passed off to their progeny, including my father, as "white" women who "drank too much coffee." Pratt encourages us to rethink the idea of "my money," to "rethink the idea that what we make or acquire is exclusively ours to control, to rethink the idea of _mine._"[105] The social labor our money represents is not ours alone but includes the labor of all those who have contributed to our class position, including our families. We need to learn more about the others whose years of heartbreaking work supported the status of our families. They are part of the reason that we occupy this particular section within our country's class structure. They are the ones to whom we are indebted.

How Elites Are Vulnerable and Damaged

It is a myth that only those in subordinate groups are hurt by the status quo. However many unearned advantages that people in the professional/managerial sector enjoy in the capitalist system, they, too, experience class vulnerability. They are hurt economically and damaged morally as the following discussion illuminates.

Like that of other workers in our class, the labor of the professional sector is made into a commodity, "thingafied," or made into a means for another's end. Fueled not only by the need to make a profit but also by the need to control, the de-skilling and the overall degradation of work are an ongoing process occurring across *all* occupational lines.[106] Like the lower tiers of the working class, many managers and professionals have been let go as the upper-class owners of unregulated technology and capital mobility make more profits without their hired hands. The corporate downsizings of the 1990s turned against blue-collar workers and people in the front office as well. Corporations such as GE, GM, Boeing, and IBM destroyed millions of high-wage jobs in the 1990s by exporting work to low-wage countries.[107] For example, corporations can get people with Ph.D.'s in computer engineering in China, India, Russia, or the Czech Republic at a fraction of the cost of U.S. professionals.[108] Given the increasing vulnerability of the majority of workers, managers are in less demand because fewer workers need direct supervision in order to produce more.[109] Other signs of the erosion in the upper working class include the fact that recent college graduates have begun to seek jobs on auto assembly lines. The U.S. Dept. of Labor estimates that 30 percent of each new class of college graduates in the next decade will be jobless or at most underemployed.[110] Fields requiring graduate degrees, including business, law, engineering, and the humanities, have more graduates than the number of jobs available.[111] Professionals in government are also vulnerable as business uses government for its own purposes (including subsidies, military spending, export loans), but at the same time seeks to downsize and even gut government when it serves the public interest.[112]

Those in the professional/managerial sector who have managed to hang on to their jobs have done so at a price, including overwork and less control over work.[113] Given the problem of oversupply in a competitive global economy, increasing numbers in this sector of the working class will continue to experience hardship because "the top of the ladder will continue to fall if the bottom is not brought up more rapidly."[114] Political analyst William Greider writes, "For the first time in human history, though most people don't yet grasp it, a fateful connection is emerging between the first and the last. One end of the ladder (or seesaw) cannot defend its general prosperity without attending to human conditions at the other end," thus supporting the argument that solidarity is increasingly necessary. Greider says that "for masses of people in the global marketplace economic, self-interest is converging with altruism."[115]

Widespread faith in self-regulating markets is illusory in the midst of chronic oversupply. So is faith that the professional/managerial sector will continue to enjoy stability. Joan Greenbaum points out that according to the Bureau of Labor Statistics' *Occupational Outlook Handbook*, "with the exception of registered nurses and computer systems analysts, *no* job growth is projected in any higher-wage category or jobs offering the potential for full-time or semi-secure status."[116] Wage erosion and job loss, once primarily confined to the lower tiers of the working class, continue to climb steadily up the class ladder. Elites do well to ask ourselves: How long will our personal work ethic be successful against such megatrends?

Despite these trends, many in the professional class continue to place trust in the dominant view. As a set of articles in *Newsweek* shows, we continue to believe, for example, in the democratization of high finance and that "hoards of Americans" are "heavily invested" in the currently lucrative stock market.[117] *Newsweek* maintains this view throughout two articles even though buried within one of them is the observation that "the richest 10 percent . . . still owns 80 percent of the nation's stocks held by individuals" and the other 90 percent shares the rest, most of it in retirement accounts.[118] Just as we erroneously believe in the democratization of high finance, so we believe that profits are honestly made according to inexorable laws and, further, that those above us are truly paying their way. Using *Newsweek* again as a barometer of the dominant view, we are told that escalating airfares and poor air service are not "the fault of the airlines" but are "an inescapable law of supply and demand . . . [since] too many people want to fly too few planes."

Myths about airline travel are in sync with class ideology. We continue to believe that the price of a first-class ticket is not subsidized by those in coach. The dominant view that first-class folk truly cover their costs is not threatened even when we are told that US Airways made a "recent decision to squeeze coach in order to give business travelers more leg room."[119] So, too, we continue to believe that "budget cuts" are protecting "our money" from those we have been taught to believe are unworthy, when in fact these cuts lower the general standard of living for most of us by slashing programs that provide the majority with some measure of economic security.[120]

Professional/managerial elites, and those aspiring to this sector, do well to be critical of our training to admire above, scapegoat below, and blame ourselves. We need to take a thoughtful look at the commonalities of our position with those in the lower working class. Analysis of class makes it evident that those on top are supported by a pyramid below. Moreover, *far more people have a stake in securing good jobs than in maximizing profits*. Along with people in the lower working class, we also create social wealth, although capitalist discourse acknowledges our role only as consumers. *We need to better connect our contributions as well as our economic vulnerability to the same capitalist dynamics that are exploiting other working-class people, albeit with greater intensity than they are exploiting us.*[121]

Professional elites are not only vulnerable economically, but also damaged as moral and spiritual persons by this class structure. When people are "thingafied," when they are bought for their labor as if they were machines, and when they are thrown away whenever their labor no longer yields the highest possible profits, they do not enjoy full personhood. However, there is little outrage over the way most workers are treated because capitalist society is saturated by behaviors (including racist and sexist behaviors) that reflect the belief that persons are things to be manipulated for others' purposes.[122] Capitalism naturalizes injustice as "the way things are."

While some recognition exists that slavery and rape are denials of personhood, escalating patterns of child abuse, sexual violence, and poverty show that a fundamental lack of respect for the rights of people to direct their own lives is widespread in capitalist culture. Indeed, capitalist profits and the needs of the authoritarian personality depend on "thingafying" and controlling people. In addition to more gross abuses, *even the most everyday relationships are being divested of their ethical and spiritual dimensions as they are subsumed under the producer/provider and consumer/client relations of capitalism.* Sociologist Robert Bellah explains, "All the primary relationships in our society, those between employers and employees, between lawyers and clients, between doctors and patients, between universities and students are being stripped of any moral understanding other than market exchange."[123] In competitive consumer capitalism, as Catholic monk Thomas Merton once said, even love becomes a business deal.[124]

What is immoral about treating persons as things? Whether workers or consumers, persons treated as objects lose (or are denied) their fundamental bodyright, or right to control their own bodies. Also at stake is their capacity to trust others, a capacity fundamental to human well-being and to moral social relations. Social environments are able to develop trust between persons when persons feel valued primarily for who they are, not for how they meet other people's needs. Trusting relationships are essential for human survival since no one can live apart from interdependence on others. In addition to basic survival needs, the capacity to trust is essential for human flourishing and the development of empathy, cognition, and creativity.[125]

Violation of Trust—Destruction of Community

Philosopher Lawrence Mordekhai Thomas contends that "evil occurs when the moral affirmation of trust is put to the service of immorality."[126] Trust is violated, for example, when notions of equality, fairness, and labor contracts are used to mystify immoral social relations in the workplace. In the capitalist workplace, the moral affirmation of trust by workers in their employers is put in the service of oppressi_ and violence. Given the class structure in the U.S. economy, all persons are damaged by capitalist work relations which are unequal and exploitative but are promulgated as just and generally believed to be so. These work relations involve a violation of trust perpetrated by those who have the social, political, and economic power to name reality (i.e., labor contracts) in service to their immoral purposes of profit without limit and the need to control people.

As Thomas explains, what is so painful about oppressive relations is that they depend on the trust and cooperation of subordinate groups whose moral capacity to trust other human beings is then used by dominants to abuse them. Evil and the corruption of human character occur when human beings, who fundamentally need to trust others, live within exploitative social relations that violate trustworthiness while everyone pretends otherwise.[127] The corruption of character may be even more true for dominants because subordinates have often maintained their integrity by active resistance to these arrangements.

Such violations of trust, including naming unjust relations as fair, equal, or loving, separate people and place groups in opposition to one another. This situation negates spiritual needs for friendship and solidarity by destroying the basis for community. The affluent minority damage their common human decency when they make super profits off others under the guise of market exchange, the supposed engine of justice. Everyone, including elites, suffers when amassing and consuming profits substitute for community. The human spirit needs sensuous connection with others. When we live off relations that violate trust and isolate people, we become dependent not on them but on our money.

When a culture becomes obsessed with controlling others and making profits off them, we try to fill up our lack of meaningful human relationships with consumer goods. Indeed, market societies must frustrate spiritual needs for friendship and solidarity so that people will consume in an effort to compensate for their loss. However, money and possessions are poor substitutes for the fulfillment of spiritual needs. Repeated studies have shown that beyond a basic and very important level of consumption, there is little difference in people's self-reported happiness with rising amounts of income.[128] Maintaining a class elitist society necessitates "a collective failure to acknowledge the needs of the spirit."[129]

Sociologist Kenneth Westhuis agrees with this assessment, arguing that we are "not only what Herbert Spencer [said we are], a collection of acquisitive, competitive selves craving satisfaction of individual needs." We are "also . . . cooperative species-beings, craving the chance to serve."[130] Species-beings thrive only within an intricate web of social relations. The ultimate interest of each lies in promoting the interest of all. British psychiatrist Adam Phillips agrees. He writes that the desire for money and possessions is a substitute for fundamental needs for affection, respect, and self-determination. These needs can be truly satisfied only in flourishing human communities. If this is the case, as I believe it is, then we are bound to be bitterly disappointed in our capitalist quest for happiness since, as Phillips says, "money is only worth what it can actually buy."[131]

Human beings, including the professional sector, long for community as a place to experience mutual respect and to create identity as we serve and are served in caring, reciprocal relations. Our humanity is wounded and our happiness is diminished by impoverished, parasitical relations. Such relations betray friendship. They keep us in the daily grind of the individualistic, competitive rat race in which some groups live off others and economic insecurity is increasing, even for professionals at the top of the working class.

The happiness of the affluent minority is also diminished when we learn about what is really going on in capitalist relations. It is difficult to fully enjoy what we have when we realize that so many others have much less, and further that what we have is related to their impoverishment. When asked what stood in the way of her pleasure, novelist Lisa Alther responded, "A knowledge of the violence and misery many other people and animals are undergoing as I sit enjoying my petty pleasures." To the same question, writer Nancy Mairs replied, "My pleasure is marred by my awareness of all the people whose circumstances . . . prevent them from enjoying the tranquillity I treasure. . . . I worry that I derive much of my pleasure, in one way or another, at their expense."[132] Alice Walker lives with the knowledge that "we are wearing clothing that cost somebody's life," and she grieves "being accomplices to evil acts done in our name and with our h earned cash."[133] As for me, shopping, dressing, eating, and doing work I might wish to do are no longer the easy pleasures they once were.

Discovering how the class system works and how it is deeply intertwined with racism, sexism, and ecological destruction is disconcerting to elites. For one thing, we can no longer thank God for "blessings" we have actually stolen from others. Yet, if to be human is to create a moral world, then perhaps we are better off living with the discomfort. It is more human to be challenged by it than to live out our days in ignorance of the grossly immoral relations and enormous human suffering that undergird most aspects of our affluent lives. It is better to know than not to know others' suffering and our own increasing vulnerability.

Solidarity Is the Solution

The solution is solidarity. Solidarity means working together to claim a fair share of power in a class structure that impoverishes some, privileges others, and damages everyone. Solidarity from a religious perspective offers a different path to happiness than the dominant religion, that is, the worship of market consumerism and stock market profits. Solidarity affirms the spiritual need of human beings for sensuous human connection, including friendships, trusting relations, and places where no one is excluded. Solidarity expresses the communitarian ethic of biblical faith and embodies the social justice principles of church teaching. Jesus lived in solidarity, and that made subordinate groups eager to follow him.

Emanating from the bottom 90 percent, solidarity can generate a mass movement (most likely triggered by a border-crossing minority) to expand democratic struggle. For solidarity to happen, it is necessary (though not sufficient) that large sectors gain rational understanding of how the political economy works to benefit the few and keeps the majority, across diverse income, racial/ethnic, gender, and sexual orientation identities, hostage to profits without limit.

This solidarity movement needs professional persons to be clear on how we are economically vulnerable to and morally damaged by present arrangements. It needs people able to connect our private economic pain not to personal failings or scapegoated others, but to larger public structures. It needs people who are not compliant with the capitalist construction of our identities as individual consumers, but think instead in terms of our common class interests with those below. It needs affluent people who know that the success of our individual efforts is based on privileged access to resources that are becoming increasingly scarce and may disappear altogether. It needs people who understand how solidarity with the lower working class will benefit all persons across race and gender lines.[134] This kind of solidarity will be built only when fragmented sectors of the working class conceive of our interests in common class terms and become sufficiently organized to change the roles we play that promote the status quo. When we understand how systems and institutions violate religious norms and our own humanity, we seek further discernment about what actions and practices appropriately resist these systems. Furthermore, it is likely that such solidarity will depend disproportionately on white women and on men and women of color who, studies show, are most likely to support the interests of poor and lower-working-class people.[135] My guess is that solidarity will also be built disproportionately by Jews, who have always been overrepresented in movements for justice, such as the civil rights, labor, and feminist movements of recent U.S. history. Because such solidarity necessitates a vision of alternative institutions and policies, it will gain momentum only by the increasing hard work of intellectuals and activists who join community struggles with those at the work site.

It is also true that rational understanding will have to be supplemented by political work addressing the human unconscious. As will be discussed in chapter 4, feminism and gay liberation help us understand how sexual repression and the patriarchal coding of desire support the authoritarian personality and interfere with greater democracy.[136] Since morality is a cognitive-affective process, rational understanding must also draw on emotions like empathy to convey the deep connections between the self and others. Religion also is a powerful resource for moral emotions. Since feeling fundamentally alone in the world fosters belief in the rationality of greed rather than shar-ing, a solution to the class structure will be fueled by feelings of sen-suous connection with others that promote compassion for oneself and for them.

But most important of all, we create a more just society not primarily by making moral arguments or by activating moral emo-tions (though these are essential parts of the process), but by con-crete forms of resisting injustice together. The solidarity emanating from the bottom 90 percent can transform society through initial strategies that wrest power from publicly subsidized "private" mar-kets and make the capitalist class start paying its way. Changes in-clude ways of more justly compensating workers while reducing hours and improving working conditions, building a social infra-structure for everyone's security and the better integration of work, family life, and environmental well-being, initiating reparations for groups who historically have given excessively for the well-being of the affluent few, and electing governments that implement this agenda for an ever vigilant constituency.

Although we seem a long way from this vision at the moment, the moral emotions that ground common human decency have not yet been thoroughly quelled. Repeated studies have shown that most people favor deep cuts in military spending, the public funding of elections, higher consumer prices to get rid of sweatshops, and other social justice measures.[137] We deserve an economy that provides our food, clothing, and other consumer items without incurring the suf-fering and impoverishment of children, women, and poor men. We deserve jobs that do not entail the violation of trustworthiness, the violence of poverty and environmental destruction, and the abuse of our labor and dignity as human beings. Given the situation of de-creasing global demand due to the proliferation of low-wage and mechanized work, we are naive if we believe our professional jobs, which cushion some of us from the worst labor abuses, are stable and long term. Nevertheless, we deserve an economy that creates and sus-tains dignified work and economic security without violating the eco-sphere. We deserve an economy in which workers decide what to pro-duce, how to produce it, and how the surplus is to be reinvested. We deserve meaningful work that is well compensated, stable, long term, and respects the environment. We need to build institutions that reproduce this justice.

Christians especially, who have a strong ethical tradition regarding the immorality of a polarized class structure, need to find ways to help people implement their best moral convictions. Christian teaching promotes solidarity that encourages experiments with new social structures and new forms of economic organization "that are increasingly in line with . . . the needs of the weakest."[138] Biblical and church resources are important in informing practices of solidarity and resistance as Christians and other moral agents decide where to stand and what to do.

4

Constructing a Compassionate Sexuality

> Among the most effective ways of oppressing a people is through the colonization of their bodies, the stigmatizing of their desires, and the repression of their erotic energies.
>
> —Eric Rofes

The structures of gender and the sexual system are sites of interaction and conflict that are intimately connected to other structures of oppression. This chapter examines how the cultural construction of gender and the sexual system grounding it are essential to maintaining class exploitation, racism, and the destruction of the natural world. When we understand the dynamics of gender and sexuality or, as Gail Rubin coined it, "the sex/gender system,"[1] we can see better how sexual liberation for all persons is essential to a broader progressive agenda that includes economic, racial, and ecological justice. Understanding the sex/gender system helps elites see how everyone's potential for communication and justice making is distorted by this unjust social structure.

The Dynamics of Gender

In our culture, gender is polarized to serve many purposes: a sexual division of labor; the selective allocation of material, emotional, and political resources; and a popular mind-set that is comfortable with relations of domination and subordination. As we shall see, gender creates the peculiar class position of women that has yet to be adequately analyzed. The basis for maintaining the differential access to class privilege experienced by most men and women is found in the patriarchal coding of erotic desire, essential to gender formation. Erotic desire, the capacity to name and affect the world, is the basis for one's sense of entitlement (or lack thereof) to social and political power.

107

Thus, gender formation, in conjunction with class and race structures, becomes a site for repressing people's erotic energies so that a few may monopolize power in the society.

The polarization of gender is based first on a polarized notion of biological sex. Human beings are socially constructed, not necessarily biologically constructed, as either male or female. Persons born with both genitalia are considered to be at best "hormonally imbalanced," and through surgery and medication, they are forced to choose one or the other genital/hormonal system. *Even though male and female do not adequately account for human sex variation,* sex polarization is essential for the construction of a polarized gender system.[2]

Gender polarization both reinforces and is sustained by a sexual relationship system that requires heteronormativity and monogamy. Such a sexual system, in turn, reproduces males and females into "properly gendered" (heterogendered) men and women. Such men and women, especially if they are white and affluent, view dominant/subordinate relations as commonsense, including the superexploitation of most white women and people of color as well as the domination by affluent white males in economic, political, and cultural life.

The process of gender polarization is based on the division of human attributes into binary opposites. This process assigns one set of attributes (especially ability to do child care, emotional work, and superexploited labor) to most women, and another set of attributes (especially propensity for intellectual work, leadership roles in society, and better-paid work) to some men. The purpose of gender, as well as the other major social distinctions, is to allocate privilege and power to some groups at the expense of others. Persons identified as the female sex are socially constructed as women so that they will provide free and unlimited child care, domestic work, and other emotional labor, and provide with other subordinate groups the superexploited wage labor in the society. Persons identified as biologically male are socially constructed as men so that some men can have dominance over other men in economic, political, familial, and reproductive matters, and all men, to greater or lesser degrees, can have dominance over at least some women. It is also true that race and class privilege may override the typical gender dynamics so that some women exercise social, political, and economic dominance over other women and some men.

The experiences of gender are multiple because gender is further stratified by structures of class and race and other intersecting differences that have evolved historically. The gender oppression experienced by poor women of color who are lesbian is *qualitatively* different from the gender oppression experienced by white affluent heterosexual women. Otherwise said, privilege in the class and race systems softens the impact of gender subordination for some women, while subordination in these systems intensifies gender oppression. Similarly, gender privilege is intensified for some men and diminished for others, depending on their class and race positions.

Women of color have reminded white feminists that isolating gender allows some women to ignore their class and race privilege. They have challenged white feminists by developing theory that shows how race, class, sexual orientation, and able-bodiedness or disability can deeply qualify the experience of gender identity.[3] Philosopher Ann Ferguson observes that at least ten race- and class-stratified genders have been identified, and these different racial and class genders do not agree on what counts as primary sources of oppression.[4] For example, even though African American women suffer race and gender subordination, these are not equal forms of oppression in a white racist society. Given the harsh realities experienced by African American men, including the fact that only 55 percent of African American men are now in the labor force, African American women gain more economically by changing their race rather than their sex/gender.[5]

While there is no common experience of gender for women as a group, gender does have meaning. For example, all women, regardless of their class or race privilege, have to struggle for civil rights. Furthermore, the patriarchal sex/gender system, as well as the race system, has been thoroughly harnessed by the class system to serve its purposes. In fact, this has been so completely accomplished that class is now the material basis for all people's oppression.

Gender and Economic Power

Given that most women work unpaid in the home and do disproportionate amounts of superexploited labor outside the home, a major function of gender polarization is to make most women work harder than the men in their class and race group. Through gender formation, women and men contribute in different ways to the reproduction of class society. At the same time, as we have said, since gender subordination is intensified by race and class subordination, and diminished by class and race privilege, different constructions of gender also divide women.

Most women are constructed not only to work at low-wage labor but also to monopolize domestic labor. Domestic labor is the cooking, cleaning, and nurturing work required to reproduce class society, that is, exploited labor power and the capitalist class itself. For most women, unshared domestic labor is work they must do in addition to wage labor. Their work provides unpaid and unlimited care and maintenance for current workers (usually male partners) as well as reproduces and maintains new workers (children).

In addition, some women are situated outside the industrial wage relation. Their labor reproduces superexploitable lower-working-class workers in their own domestic spheres as well as upper-working-class exploitable labor in the professional households where they work.[6] A relatively few women and the women they hire through their class and race privilege work to reproduce and maintain the capitalist class itself. Consequently, through various race- and class-stratified ways of subordinating women, the capitalist class keeps the maintenance and replacement of exploitable labor power, as well as the reproduction of the capitalist class itself, as cost effective as possible. Polarized gender formation reproduces and maintains workers and capitalists for free for the capitalist class.

Clearly, the more privileged a woman is, the less she endures gender subordination. The more class and race privilege she has, the less she contributes to the material labor of reproducing class society. Through her position of privilege, she can exploit the labor of more subordinate women (and men) to do this gender work for her. The most privileged women do not do domestic labor or wage labor. Their class and race dominance eliminates most, not all, of the subordination that comes with gender. However, while the most privileged women can more or less divest themselves of gender subordination, they do this at the expense of the intensified gender subordination of other women.

Most women participate with greater or lesser degree of severity in gender subordination. The majority of women of all races do all or most of domestic labor and engage in superexploited wage labor as well. Although all workers are exploited in the class system, women's free and unlimited domestic labor serves as the basis for women's disproportionate representation in the superexploited tiers of the working class. Here the majority of women labor in low-paying, stressful jobs, which are public extensions of unpaid housework.

Thus, gender polarization requires most women to work a double day: the first day for patriarchy and capitalism, and the second for capitalism. Some women use their class and race privilege to exploit other women to do one or both days for them. Properly gendered women work the first shift for patriarchy when they provide men with more leisure, more nurturance, more sex, and more domestic services at home than women themselves usually receive. They also work the first shift for capitalism by reproducing and maintaining the workforce for free. Women work the second shift for capitalism by doing wage work and keeping wages low, due to their unpaid labor at home. One could argue that women support patriarchy on the second shift, as well, by giving men more opportunity for the better-paying jobs.

In terms of women's peculiar class status, working a double day means that most women support capitalism in the home as well as at work in ways that do not apply to most men. Consequently, no matter what class position women may share with men in the public sphere, women's additional position as a domestic laboring class gives them a different position from men in the overall class structure. No successful formula has yet been found that analyzes the class position of women in relation to that of men.[7]

Women's position as a domestic laboring class has enormous ramifications for their access to economic and political power. As I have said, this double shift for most women is the basis for women's disproportionate presence in the lower rungs of the labor market, including jobs that are public extensions of housework. In the United States in the early 1990s, women as a group increased their median earnings from 65.2 to 74.0 percent of what men made in wages. As discussed in chapter 3, the increase was primarily due to a decline in men's earnings as the labor market lost better-paying jobs to foreign investment, downsizing, mechanization, and proliferating low-wage work. Even so, U.S. men hold almost twice the amount of wealth that women do, and women's poverty rate in the United States is more than twice that of men.[8]

In addition, racism affects women's labor in that government statistics show that in 1992, 21.1 percent of white women, 26.9 percent of black women, and 36.6 percent of Latinas earned less than $13,091 for year-round full-time work.[9] Racism affects high-earning women in that 3.8 percent of white women, 1.6 percent of black women, and 1.8 percent of Latinas earned above $52,364 in 1992 for year-round full-time work.[10] Since 1992 the wage inequality among women of different racial groups has only deepened. From 1992 to 1997, when the economy grew by 6.7 percent, the typical (or median) white woman worker's wages grew by only 1.4 percent. In the same period, however, the typical black woman worker *lost* 2.1 percent in wages and the typical Latina *lost* 6.5 percent in wages. College-educated white women saw their wages increase between 1992 and 1997 by 4.4 percent, while college-educated black women *lost* 3.2 percent in wages and college-educated Latinas *lost* 1 percent in wages during this economic growth period.[11] It is clear that racism affects women workers in that "black women are still more likely than white women to be paid less, to be unemployed, to be supervised rather than to supervise."[12]

The deeply gendered and racialized nature of the political economy is seen not only in the racially stratified and gendered division of unpaid labor and sex-segmented labor markets, but also in gender-structured social welfare policy.[13] Here men receive "entitlements" such as veterans' benefits and unemployment insurance, whereas women receive "handouts" such as welfare. The need for welfare policy, or "public patriarchy" as it has also been called, has deepened in recent decades as men have lost economic ground in late capitalism and, therefore, their "marriageability." As familial patriarchy has declined and families have grown more dependent on women's lower-wage work, public patriarchy in the form of state intervention in the family has increased. Sexism also increases as women are targeted as the problem for family instability and social deterioration created by advanced capitalism. Public patriarchy enlists professional-sector women among the doctors, welfare workers, public health nurses, child psychologists, and social workers who often infantalize women from the lower tiers of the working class and remind them of their intellectual, emotional, and physical inferiority.[14]

While capitalism largely harnesses male dominance for its purposes, it is true that capitalism works to erode patriarchy. Women's increasing representation in the labor market means that some women are able to have real choices about marriage. Due to the inroads of wage labor, people's greater opportunity to live outside the traditional family has been a major impetus for the recognition of lesbian and gay sexual orientation and the gay liberation movement.[15] Nevertheless, the class system also "softens women up" for men. Given that about 78 percent of full-time women workers earn $25,000 a year or less, most women with children do not have the financial resources to live independently from men. Laws and other public policies intensify this heterosexist situation when marriage, rather than citizenship, is used to distribute such resources as tax, health, and housing benefits.[16]

In global terms, the class gap between women and men is even greater than in the Unites States. Ethicist Daniel Maguire quotes a United Nations report, which states that "women constitute 70 percent of the world's 1.3 billion absolute poor, own less than 1 percent of the world's property, but work two-thirds of the world's working hours."[17] Drawing on the work of philosopher-economist Amartya Sen, Meera Nanda says that "women are poorer than their male counterparts in all socioeconomic groups . . . because of culturally determined consensus about their 'worth' that determines their relative access to the available goods and resources, both material . . . and cultural." Nanda reminds us that "all members of even the poorest families are not equally poor."[18]

Despite these enormous constraints, women have been active around the globe in resistance to exploitation and oppression. Hazel Carby studied the diversity of twentieth-century women's struggles, including the Igbo women in Nigeria against British colonialism; black women's leadership against land seizures in Africa, Latin America, and the Caribbean; the long history of fighting against unpaid and wage labor by women in India; and the organized struggles of Asian women in Britain, not only against male-dominated capitalism but against white women employers as well.[19] Women of color in the United States have relied on female networks and the extended family in their daily struggles for survival, revealing that family, though often oppressive, can be a powerful resource for some women. Class- and race-stratified gender creates not only victims but also creative resisters.

The political economy in both its privatized and its public spheres uses gender polarization to give some men numerous privileges and power not available to most women. Because women also constitute a domestic laboring class that serves both patriarchy and capitalism, women belong to a different class group than can be accounted for in traditional class theory. However, given that women disproportionately share the worst wage-labor exploitation with some men, women's poverty is deeply rooted in the class structure as well as the structures of gender and race.

Although there is no common experience of gender oppression since gender is so deeply stratified by race and class, gender oppression does have meaning. However much the experience of gender is mediated through the superexploitation of women in public work, for example, it is also true that male supremacist relations in family nurture, domestic work, and sex have persisted through different modes of production such as those in the former Soviet Union, China, and Cuba. However much the experience of gender is mediated through race or class, in all male-dominant societies women, because they are women, are expected to serve and care for the men and children in their race, class, and kinship group.[20]

Gender, Eros, and Cultural Power

As the basis for the exploitation and oppression of women in domestic labor and wage work, a polarized gender structure constructs women differently from men through the patriarchal and capitalist shaping of erotic desire. Christian ethicist Beverly Harrison defines the erotic as our power to identify, name, sensuously connect with, and affect our world. The erotic is the source of our energy and all our doing. It is the opposite of numbness and passivity. Harrison explains that erotic energy emanates from living deeply in our bodies and being able to

discern what we feel. Erotic energy empowers us to become subje
of our own lives, to be moral agents as we create mutual relationship
in sensuous connection with one another and the natural world.[21]

I agree with Harrison and would like to name my experience of
the erotic. This is a difficult task since words always fall short of the
experience. Being pressed, I would say that the erotic has to do with
intensity of engagement, a heightened sense of excitement, awareness
of one's ability to affect others, a deepened sense of vulnerability, and
the need to express joy and gratitude. Erotic experiences with my and
others' children, with women and men I love, with the ocean or the
forest, while writing or running or teaching, are whole-body, whole-
heart, and whole-soul experiences. Erotically empowered, I am as aware
of the other as I am intensely aware of myself. I live completely in
the present moment and am totally absorbed in the sensuousness of
the person, environment, or activity that commands my attention and
resources. I wish to touch, move with, feel with, be forever with the
other. In the erotic moment, consciousness of all else is gone. The
present is all there is in this world and all I want ever to be. The fact
that some would call my experience of the sensuous erotic a "mystical
experience" demonstrates the inadequacy of a dualistic worldview that
separates the material world from spiritual reality.

The erotic experience makes me feel power intensely shared with
others. I am deeply assured that I have power to make a difference in
others' lives, even as my sense of vulnerability to their power is heightened. I need others to care for and about me. And I sense that I am as
vital to their well-being as they are to mine. I find such mutuality
exhilarating. Because the erotic mediates to me the fullness of being
alive, both in my ability to impact others and in my joy in being trea-
sured by them, I feel gratitude and joy. Fully empowered, I wish to
pass on my power and fullness of being to others. Marvin Ellison
sums it up: "Erotic power [is] a significant moral power, making intimacy possible between people and their world."[22] Erotic power, then,
has to do with shared power, with heightened awareness of self and
others, with cherishing vulnerability even as we increase energy for
doing. In this, the erotic is our power for justice making, our power
for creating right relations with ourselves, others, and the world that
sustains us.

Under the system of patriarchal domination, however, eros must be considerably distorted for purposes of social control, exploitation, and oppression. Dominants especially target women and other groups who, like women, are overassociated with their bodies and their supposed inferiority. If these groups are socialized to repress eros, they are disempowered for purposes of maintaining the unjust relations of the status quo. Drawing on the work of Patricia Hill Collins, Ellison contends that our social system has a fear of deep feeling and of our tendency as species-beings to connect with one another. Our capacity to identify across diversity and engage in an expansive "big love" must be denied. For monopolized power to be sustained, power-sharing erotic energy must be distorted, that is, we must be disempowered and disconnected from ourselves and others.[23]

In patriarchy, eros has been harnessed to the need of producing heirs and narrowed to a focus on male-dominant genital sex and reproduction. Under systems of male dominance, women have had to give up the control of their bodies to fathers, husbands, and other male authorities who monopolized power in other areas of life as well. Patriarchy seeks to divest women (and men of subordinate class and racial/ethnic groups) not only of their economic power, but of their sexual and political power as well.

Part of regulating sexuality is to racialize it. In opposition to sexualized racism, discussed below, "good women" have been constructed as "white." To be white means to be without sexual desire or to have sexual desire only for husbands who require their monogamy. This exclusive ownership has been necessary so that propertied men could control women and their reproductive powers, for purposes of inheritance. Patriarchal men have traditionally not been bound by monogamy. While Christian and other forms of religious marriage, as well as secular marriage in contemporary liberal societies, have supported monogamy for men, men have usually operated under the cultural permission of the double standard and the widespread belief that "boys will (and should) be boys."

Men have reinforced women's lack of bodyright, including the absence of cultural permission to exercise sexual desire or be in touch with a sense of political, economic, or social entitlement by escalating rates of physical, emotional, and sexual abuse. Rape, sexual harassment, and other forms of violence against women are on the rise everywhere. The domestic sphere where most women labor for numerous unpaid hours is often the most dangerous place for women. In the United States, a woman is beaten in her home every fifteen seconds, and at least one in every ten perpetrators is a man from the professional sector.[24] In addition, between one in five and one in seven U.S. women will be the victims of a completed rape.[25]

One quarter to more than half of women in many countries of the world have been physically abused by a present or former partner.[26] Given the prevalence of violence in women's lives, *the threat of which affects all women*, there is a remarkable lack of attention to how this violence damages women's sexuality and self-esteem, including women's sense of entitlement to bodyright and social power. If eros is the site of our personal power and passionate connection to the world, the patriarchal narrowing of eros to genital sex and the distorting of sexuality into a site of danger rather than pleasure do not bode well for the empowerment and well-being of women.

In addition to the patriarchal coding of sexual desire, the capitalist coding of desire further narrows the erotic for men as well as women. The implications of capitalist eros are also significant for race privilege. As discussed earlier, the disciplined capitalist workplace requires an industrial morality that represses the human capacity for sensuous connection with oneself, one's labor, other people, and the natural world. Playful people who enjoy leisure and a more spontaneous sexuality are not good for business. They threaten those whose need is to exercise managerial control at the work site. As a result of the capitalist manipulation of human eroticism, the patriarchal focus on a regulated marriage ethic and male genital sexuality has only intensified in the service of capitalist interests. The erotic has been harnessed to the service of the work ethic, reproduction, and the selling of products.[27]

People who enjoy socially useful and self-gratifying sensuous work do not flourish under the strict routines, repetitive nature, and antiseptic (or dangerous) environments of capitalist work. For example, in their efforts to get the most out of exploited labor power, capitalists in the early twentieth century developed the "science of work." In this process they "investigated and redefined the relationship between

machine and human being to allow for the 'calibration' of workers—
the 'mechanical' fine-tuning of their bodies—to fit them to machin-
ery."[28] The erotic as genital supremacy confined to the home becomes
even more necessary as bodies are transformed into desexualized
machines of public labor and means to profits in the marketplace.

Historically, the patriarchal focus on male genital sex became
harnessed to the service of reproducing class society as it kept upper
working class women in the home to bear and raise the next genera-
tion of workers. Even today, highly regulated and narrowed eros, in
which people have cultural permission for sex only within heterosexual monogamous marriage, serves capitalism by generating surplus eros that can be mobilized for profit making. Unmet erotic
desire is used to sell products as well as to create new commodities
that can be sold for profit. These include the enormously lucrative
global corporate businesses of prostitution and pornography. The
sex industries function as safety valves for repressed and distorted
eros. In addition, because of antisex taboo, these industries involve a
lower-paid, more vulnerable labor force, which guarantees a higher
profit margin.[29]

Capitalist culture deals with unmet erotic desire in ways that also
promote racism. As discussed in chapter 2, at root racism is a cultural
construct tied to attitudes, behaviors, and social patterns that are anti-
poor and erotophobic. Given highly regulated (white) sexuality, unmet
erotic desire is channeled not only into consumption but also into
scapegoating. The racial identities of men and women of color, as
well as Jewish people and even white working-class people, have been
constructed, in varying degrees, to carry the negative body and the
rejected sexuality of whites. White religious prohibitions against sensuality, along with the rigid sexual regulation in (white) industrial
morality, have turned people of color, their bodies, music, and other
cultural elements into dangerous carriers of the erotic as forbidden
sensuality.[30] Whites project their fascination about forbidden sexuality onto people of color who become "exotic." They also project loathing about sexuality, carefully learned, onto scapegoated others, who
become dangerous and in need of white social control.

Those who carry the negative body, especially communities of
color, white Jews, and gay people, are caricatured as sexual preda-

tors. Jewish people become "carnal," lesbians and gay men become "pedophiles," black men become "rapists," black women and working-class white women become "whores," always ready for sex, and poor women of color become "promiscuous welfare cheats." White women, or more accurately, those wishing to achieve white normative status, must present themselves as devoid of sexual desire, except for their "marital duty." Thus, the gendered, racist construction of sexual desire divides "good" (white) women from most "promiscuous" women of color since "good" women do not have sexual desire, but enjoy being submissive and compliant to men. Historian Evelyn Brooks Higginbotham suggests, "Gender identity is inextricably linked to and even determined by racial identity."[31] And, we might add, racism is inextricably tied to those who carry the disrespected sexual body.

On the other hand, properly gendered men with class and race privilege have cultural permission for sexual desire and are socialized to feel entitled to sex with women. They feel especially justified in sexual entitlement to women of color, and to a lesser extent poor white women, because such women are viewed as not properly gendered and therefore always "ready for sale."[32] Since men of color and white Jewish men are often viewed as oversexed rivals, white men must protect "their" women from them. Sexualized racism is used to justify eroticized violence, including the rape of women of color, and such practices as lynching African Americans in order to control subordinates who might be tempted to resist.

As more women live outside marriage, as lesbians and gay men become more visible in their demands, and as more men lose marriageability in the radically restructured economy, patriarchy is waging a war against these capitalist inroads to its traditional forms of gender privilege. This conflict is especially seen in the obsession with family values and increasing emphasis on both gender polarization and heterosexual monogamy. In this climate, gender privilege in sexuality can be overruled by the racist coding of sexuality. As legal scholar Patricia Williams explains, "Race is less about biology than cultural imagination." Williams agrees with novelist Toni Morrison's assessment that Bill Clinton, a saxophone player who engaged in adult consensual sex outside marriage, has failed to fully re "white" racial status in the society. Williams describes Clinton ...ewered with all the tropes of blackness" because, in Morrison's words, he is the product of a "single parent household, born poor, working-class," whose body, whose privacy, and whose "unpoliced sexuality became the focus of persecution."[33] A U.S. president can sign a 1996 welfare bill that cuts billions of dollars to poor legal immigrants, low-income disabled children, working-poor families, and the elderly poor, and dismantles a sixty-year legacy of federal responsibility for other poor families, and people yawn. However, when nonmarital sex occurs in the White House, we have the second impeachment trial in U.S. history.

The gendered and racist coding of sexual desire has enormous ramifications for people's sense of personal power and entitlement in society. *Those who endure the weight of a deviant sexuality as well as those who are not supposed to have sexual desire at all are regulated at the central site of their personal power.* Their desires as moral agents are not only discounted; they are seen as dangerous and in need of control for purposes of social order. Their capacities for sensuous labor, for naming reality from their point of view, and for deep connections to others threaten the status quo. Therefore, the patriarchal and racist coding of desire must eroticize inequality as it increases fear and enforces conformity to all the systems of oppression. White class-elitist men have been allowed, even encouraged, to have privileged access to the labor and sexuality of subordinate others who are the majority of the population. For everyone else sexual expression, and personal power, is highly regulated. It is centered on the expectation of heterosexuality and monogamy, or highly restricted sexual entitlement, especially for those who wish to achieve properly gendered female and normative "white" racial status in the society. Theologian Mary Pellauer asks, "What stirs in our orgasms, that there should be so many obstacles around them?"[34]

Heterosexual monogamy, and the gender polarization necessary to reproduce it, is so invested in patriarchal, capitalist, and racist interests that our sexual system cannot sustain clear boundaries between sexual intimacy and sexual violence. For example, many don't know how to separate flirting from behavior that escalates into harassment and humiliation. Neither can the sexual system sustain boundaries between fidelity in relationship and monopoly ownership of a partner's body and sexual, emotional, and physical resources. In recent times, there has been less cultural permission for the double standard for men as intimacy relations become even more tightly bound to the system of property relations.[35]

Even though women's experiences of sexual disempowerment vary according to class and race, gender oppression in this area as well as in the class system does have meaning. In all male-dominant societies women have struggled relentlessly for control over their sexual and reproductive functions, and most women have had little or no control. Men within the dominant class and race groups have been socialized to expect entitlement to women's bodies, including legal control over them. Catholic ethicist Christine Gudorf characterizes women's relative lack of sexual and reproductive choice as a violation of bodyright, which is foundational to the full personhood and moral agency of all human beings.[36] Former psychoanalyst Alice Miller likens the enforced divorce between the self and one's inner desires to "soul murder."[37]

Gender has meaning because in all male-dominant societies, cultural permission is granted for sex only if it is between a man and a woman within the institution of marriage or a similar form of ownership pattern. In male-dominant societies, men are socialized to demand entitlement over (at least some) women's physical and emotional labor as well as their sexual services.[38] Women do not have cultural permission for sexual desire or sexual agency. In capitalist, racist, male-dominant societies men have cultural permission to punish the women—and men—whose sexual desire is deviant by virtue of not having achieved female or "white" normative status, or by virtue of being gay, or even by virtue of having been raped.

While women suffer gender subordination differently (and men wage gender dominance differently) according to race and class, all women suffer from a lack of equality with the men in their group. While women participate differently in the unpaid and wage labor aspects of gender subordination, as well as in permission or persecution for sexual desire, "all women suffer disadvantage in the political sphere."[39] All women, even capitalist class women, must struggle for equal rights in the society.

It Has Not Always and Everywhere Been So

Leslie Feinburg argues that most people subscribe to the "Flintstone" school of anthropology. They believe that social change is not really possible because the way we are now is the way things have always been.[40] Despite popular belief, it simply is *not* true that gender-polarized men and women are what being human is always about. It simply is *not* true that heterosexuality and monogamy have always had normative status in every culture's sexual ethics. Anthropological study provides evidence that our notions of biological sex, gender, and heterosexuality are socially produced. Historically and culturally, gender is much larger in human experience than the "heterogender" that supports heteronormativity. "Properly gendered" (heterogendered) males and females, heterosexuality, monogamy, or even biological maleness or femaleness is not a natural or universal human condition.

As mentioned previously, persons in Western culture born without clear differentiation into one of the two socially defined biological sexes have been forced to choose whether they wished to live as socially constructed (heterogendered) men or women. However, this has not been the view of all societies. For example, the Dine (Navajo) nation in North America viewed persons born with both male and female genitalia not as imbalanced and in need of correction, but as examples of human completeness.[41]

We see especially how biological sex, maleness and femaleness, is socially constructed to support heterogender when we consider the struggle of transgendered people. Transgendered people wish to express themselves as a gender different from the gender the culture has attached to their biological sex. Called such names as transvestites, transsexuals, drag queens, and cross-dressers, they are considered gender outlaws. In male-dominant, racist, capitalist societies, biological females whose self-expression is "masculine" or males whose self-expression is "feminine" are mistakenly assumed to *always* be stereotyped lesbian or gay, and they are subject to everything from harassment to violence to murder. Yet there is a whole range of ways for biological males and females to express themselves.[42] Many possible configurations exist between biological sex, gender expression, and sexual practice.

In societies that do not need a polarized gender structure to support heteronormativity and its vested economic and political interests, transgendered people have expressed their gender without derision and violence, and they have been honored. The colonial invaders named transgendered people, thought to have flourished in more than 135 North American Indian nations, *berdache*. Honored as shamans, great warriors, or the highest-ranking members of governing councils, the *berdache* were tortured and burned at the stake by Christian invaders. The economic, social, and political values of European Christians made incomprehensible these powerful leaders of their societies—male women, female men, and bisexed, bigendered, and bisexual individuals.[43]

Moreover, societies that do not need a polarized gender structure and heteronormativity do not enforce monogamy. Caribbean slaves ridiculed the new slave codes of the 1780s, which promulgated European marriage to encourage the local breeding of slaves. They wished, to the contrary, to continue their practice of each man and woman living together for as long or as short as they pleased. Caldecott, a nineteenth-century church historian, said of this situation, "There is in the Negro race a nearer approach to equality between the sexes than is found in the European races."[44] However, Europeans perceived equality between the sexes, the independence of women, and the disinterest of men in sexual control (and militarism) as signs of primitive backwardness and racial inferiority that needed to be eradicated.

The work of anthropologists Peggy Reeves Sanday, David Levinson, and H. P. Phillips shows that societies that do not enforce regulated sexual desire have egalitarian relations between the sexes and little violence.[45] Sanday found in 47 percent of 156 tribal societies that violence, including rape, is rare when gender polarization, racism, and other hierarchical differences are not present in the society.[46] David Levinson found that gender-based violence was virtually absent in 16 out of 90 peasant and small-scale societies. In the work of H. P. Phillips, the Central Thai were especially noteworthy for their disdain of aggression and their highly developed methods of conflict resolution. Among the Central Thai, divorce was common, men were as likely as women to engage in domestic labor and child care, and women were as likely as men to manage the family business.[47] Cross-cultural studies provide ample evidence that domineering males are as socially onstructed as submissive females. Male conditioning, not the condition of being male, is at the heart of male dominance.

Multiple studies provide evidence that lack of erotic regulation and freedom in gender and sexual expression are important for social peace. Using the massive cross-cultural research of neurophysiologist James W. Prescott, ethicist James Nelson points out that sex-positive and body-positive societies that allow a great deal of touching and physical nurturance are predictably cooperative, peaceful societies. It is no wonder that male violence is so prevalent in gender-polarized, racist, capitalist societies where sexuality is highly regulated and presumed sinful until proven innocent. Nelson says, "Body-selves deprived of pleasure become both angry and deadened. They search for violent ways of making themselves feel alive."[48]

Gender fluidity and fluidity in sexual practice threaten an economy that depends on the heterosexual monogamous family as the linchpin of other oppressive structures. These include the sexual division of labor, the oppression of people of color, and the monopolization of economic and political power by the privileged few. Indeed, many scholars have argued that the origin of the monogamous, heteronormative family lies in the evolution of society into polarized classes based on the private ownership of property. Kinship systems based on the property rights of a relatively few privileged men necessitated the subordination of women, children, slaves, and other men without property.[49] Leslie Feinburg concludes, "In reality it was the rise of private property, the male-dominant family and class divisions that led to narrowing what was considered acceptable self-expression."[50]

To understand the particular sex/gender system that so deeply shapes our humanity, we must see how heteronormativity and compulsory heterosexual monogamy (marriage) serve specific interests. Since sexual expression must be highly regulated for the purpose of maldistributing economic benefits and political power, it stands to reason, as studies confirm, that heteronormativity and monogamy are neither natural nor universal. As we have seen, heteronormativity is, in fact, the organizing institution for achieving two unequal genders conceived as "opposite." Heteronormativity includes the material deprivation and political disempowering of women as a group, lesbians and gay people, people of color, working-class and working-poor people, and others who as groups are not properly heterogendered and are overidentified with their (supposedly deviant) sexuality.

Outside a sex/gender system constructed to serve male-dominant, class-stratified, racist interests, compulsory heterosexual monogamy is not needed. *Heterogender, heteronormativity, and monogamy exist not because they are natural to the human condition, but because they are needed to support the one interlocking system of patriarchal, racist capitalism.* Chrys Ingraham asks, "Without institutionalized heterosexuality—that is, the ideological and organizational regulation of relations between men and women—would gender even exist?"[51]

I think fluid and evolving gender expression will always exist for purposes of varied self-expression. But certainly without a race-stratified class society, severe gender polarization would have considerably less social support. When we understand how essential gender polarization is, not only to the reproduction of male dominance, but to other forms of hierarchy and social stratification, we will understand the inability of most people to imagine an alternative sex/gender system.

The gender system is the first and most powerful experience people have of unshared power. Deeply ingrained into the social world of children, the gender-polarized heterosexual family teaches them that dominant/subordinate relations are normal and natural. People raised in sexist environments believe that men's entitlement and women's self-sacrifice are necessary expressions of human love and essential to the right ordering of society. *People raised in gender-polarized families are conditioned to accept race hierarchies, abject poverty, and arrogant affluence as the way the world naturally is.* People conditioned to accept gender hierarchy have little trouble with white supremacy and with the reality that some groups suffer economic exploitation and cultural marginalization to the benefit of others. People raised in heterogendered, monogamous families understand intimate relations as property relations. They believe it is only right and just that parents exercise ownership rights over children for whom the community is not responsible, and that a partner is the source of their personal supply of emotional and sexual resources over which they should have monopoly control.

With the sex/gender system serving so many functions, it is no wonder that people with more fluid gender expressions or sexual practices attract fear, loathing, and social ire. They threaten the foundations of the whole social (dis)order. Liberation efforts waged by some heterosexual women, gays, lesbians, transgendered people, and their allies to interfere with the polarized gender structure and reconstruct the traditional family threaten to destabilize society when they challenge this foundational system.

The problem, however, is not the breakdown of the family; the problem is the traditional family itself. The reason the nuclear family is breaking down—or exists as one of the most dangerous sites in North America for women and children—is because people in it are often isolated emotionally and stressed economically. The real problem is the capitalist family structure, which is based on ownership patterns and is in service to the system of profit making.

As we have seen, there are many societies, primarily societies of color, with different sex/gender systems and different constructions of family. British social theorist Hazel Carby cautions, however, that better-looking social relations in alternative systems may not mean that women and others are not oppressed. Assessments from outsiders cannot determine what is important to the people themselves in these societies.[52] U.S. historian Howard Zinn is also aware of the dangers of romanticizing. Nevertheless, his reading of the historical record is that Europeans "were not coming into an empty wilderness but into a world which in some places was as deeply populated as Europe itself, where the culture was complex, where human relations were more egalitarian than in Europe, and where the relations among men, women, children and nature were more beautifully worked out than perhaps any place in the world."[53] Despite our "Flintstone" perceptions of gender and sexual ethics, it seems clear that patriarchal and capitalist systems have created a historically bounded sexual morality and system of family relations that would hardly be credited with much moral wisdom by many societies.

How Elites Are Hurt

All women, at least to some degree, suffer from our sex/gender system. This system makes women responsible for more work than the men in their group. Many women are forced to work harder than other women and most men. Apart from their actual sexual practice, the sex/gender system punishes women for sexual deviance because of their race or ethnicity, social class or sexual orientation. It also gives cultural permission to punish even women with class and race privilege who claim sexual desire outside monogamous patterns. And it makes the denial of equal political rights to all women seem commonsense.

Our sex/gender system also gives cultural permission to discriminate against or punish the men who, like women, are overidentified with their bodies and a presumed deviant sexuality. These include white Jewish men, men of color, gay men, working-class and working-poor men, whites who have not achieved "white" normative status, and disabled men. However, dominants also suffer, including race- and class-privileged heterosexual males. Their children suffer, too, because the family care system is collapsing across the socioeconomic spectrum.

It is a mistake to think that our sex/gender system does not hurt class- and race-privileged men. Like most men, privileged men are socially constructed by the ideology of masculine dominance to repress many of their human capacities. This repression is necessary for such men to become aggressive and seek control over women and as many men as possible. Privileged men rely less on personal forms of aggression, such as harassment, battering, and rape, because they have more deadly forms of violence at their disposal, such as unshared economic and political power.

Privileged men, like most men, are socialized to deny certain emotions, especially the pain and humiliation they feel from men who have authority over them. Most males at some point in their lives are harassed, intimidated, humiliated, and abused into being properly gendered men. They are pressured to conform to certain stereotypes and play certain roles or else stand in danger of losing their manhood. These roles include making fun of women and the emotional work required to bring about relationships of mutuality and reciprocity. They include aspiring to (uncritical) leadership in a violent society that promotes war and readiness for war, makes "killings" in the market the highest expression of human achievement, prevents people from meeting basic needs, and destroys the environment.

Male gender formation carefully sets up privileged men for this
task as it deprives them of the human skills for relationship and
nurturance. Educator Paul Kivel observes that "it takes years and years
of training to make boys into violent men."[54] In short, privileged men
are hurt because, like most men, they are truncated people without
access to their full human capacities. One could argue that many privileged men are more morally compromised than other less-powerful
men because if they want to maintain their power, they must perpetrate or support those who perpetrate the most massive forms of violence in the society.

The privileged are also hurt when we look at what is going on at
home. In constructing men who are largely undeveloped or underdeveloped in the human potential for nurturance, and in forcing most
women to seek wage labor, the sex/gender system of racist, capitalist
patriarchy is placing the well-being of increasing numbers of children
in jeopardy. This includes the children of privileged groups as more
upper-income parents spend more time in the workplace, and as quality child care becomes scarce and expensive.

With parents spending less time at home, children are increasingly vulnerable, especially if men are unable or unwilling to do domestic labor. In her extensive studies of domestic labor, sociologist
Arlie Hochschild has found increasing stress in the home. She discov-
ered that many affluent parents are not opting to work part-time, that
upper-income new mothers are not any more likely to stay home after three months than low-income new mothers, that job culture dis-
parages parents who put children first, and that quality time in the
home is becoming like an office appointment.[55]

Hochschild and coresearcher Anne Machung found that only
21 to 30 percent of men who make more or the same wages as wives
share the domestic labor of caring for children. Men who make more
money than their partners are *less* likely to do so.[56] Men lose out because the relatively few men heavily involved with their children were
significantly happier with their family life than less-involved men, and
there is some evidence that their children were more empathetic than
other children.[57] The fact remains, however, that women who constitute almost half of those who do public labor are responsible for *at
least* 70 to 80 percent of domestic labor in the United States today.

As to be expected, Hochschild and Machung reported that the majority of fathers give child care responsibility to mothers, mothers are increasingly giving it to other, more subordinate women. Baby-sitters and child-care center workers are often under pressure to keep their jobs by not bothering harried parents with children's distress. In the words of the authors, "In a time of stalled revolution—when women have gone to work, but the workplace, the culture, and most of all the men have not adjusted themselves to this new reality—children can be the victims."[58] Because of men's enormous fear of nurturing and tenderness, they even more than women are tied to gender roles, to the detriment of themselves and their children.

To make matters worse for children, research indicates that as home life becomes more stressful, women as well as men are seeking refuge in the office. Hochschild says that "increasing numbers of women are discovering a great male secret—that work can be an escape from the pressures of home, pressures that the changing nature of work itself are only intensifying."[59] In other words, not only is wage labor taking up increasing amounts of parents' time, but women are being tempted to give it even more time. Given a partner unwilling to share the second shift, women do not have enough time to be truly successful at home. The loss of a domestic labor force is creating a crisis of care in this society, with the smallest, most vulnerable members paying the biggest price. As children today spend less time with adults than perhaps any other time in history, the need for quality child care unites people across class and race.

Privileged groups are also hurt, along with everyone else, by the restriction of our capacity for sensuous connection with others, especially through the system of compulsory monogamy. As we have seen, a highly regulated sexual system is one of the pillars of racist capitalism and a de-eroticized industrial morality. Monogamy channels erotic desire into a highly restricted sexual system that is often not equal to the burden.

In the latter decades of the twentieth century, divorce rates soared, peaking at one out of two marriages in the United States ending in divorce.[60] While the reasons are many, human need for nurturing touch and sensual connection cannot be satisfied by genitally focused sex or by one person exclusively. Even when monogamous relationships are rich and satisfying, they are not sufficient to compensate for the loss of erotic connection we experience elsewhere, or balm enough to heal any deep wounds to our self-respect from families of origin, the workplace, and other sites of oppression.[61] Most people need a wide variety of friendships of varying emotional intensity. Yet as the male-dominant family is eroded by the restructured economy, fear increases about unregulated sexual expression. As the economic basis for the family is weakened, the ideology of the male-dominant heterogendered family is promoted for purposes of social control. Racist, capitalist patriarchy, especially as promoted by the Religious Right, intensifies the demonization of sexual expression other than heterosexual monogamy.

Privileged people are hurt, as are most in the society, through increasing loss of access to our deepest selves. As the cultural ethos increases restrictions on sexual passion, people experience a more general shutdown of feelings and emotions. As educators Joanna Macy and Molly Brown remind us, repression cannot be isolated to certain areas of our capacity to feel. "Repression," they say, "takes a mammoth toll on our energy and also on our sensitivity to the world around us. Repression is not a local anesthetic."[62] In other words, if we must shut down in one area, we shut down at the central nervous system. If we cannot feel deep friendship including sexual passion, we cannot feel much else either, including deep joy, compassion, or pain for our world. Beverly Harrison notes the perplexity of progressive Christian activists at the growing political apathy of many in the churches and traces social passivity to the impoverished dynamics of our interpersonal, primary relationships.[63] Highly regulated male genital sexuality not only shuts down many dimensions of the erotic; it deadens our potential to be justice makers. We become numb to social pain and are unable to feel outrage about what is going on in the world. People who are good at censuring their feelings do not know what they feel and do not have access to compassion for themselves and others.

In addition, a highly restrictive sexual system intensifies authoritarianism in people's relations to themselves and others and thereby reinforces the very systems that are doing us in. As Ellison points out, when people's physical and emotional needs are not being met, when they are divorced from sensuous connection to others and the natural world, people "tend to become more repressive about sex, more judgemental about differences, and more unforgiving toward themselves and others."[64] The more deprived we are of sensuous connections to others in work and play, the more we experience scarcity and the need to protect our "supply." We increase our dependency on exceptionless rules, such as compulsory heterosexual monogamy, which keep us moral infants, unable to engage in the self-critical ethical reflection that comes with the freedom to engage deeply with others.[65]

It is important for dominants to see that compulsory heterosexual monogamy does not hurt only heterosexual women and gay, lesbian, bisexual, and transgendered people. As Nicola Field says, the sex/gender system "is a powerful weapon preventing people of all sexualities from realizing their potential, socially as well as sexually."[66] The requirement to achieve a heterogender in order to secure normative status in this society hurts most people who become truncated human beings, restricted from expressing or developing the widest possible range of human attributes. So, too, the demonization of most sexual relationships hurts most people who are told their feelings and desires are illegitimate. Any expression outside a restrictive ownership pattern may result in social, political, and/or economic punishment for any of us. All of us are damaged because eros and sexual fulfillment are essential to human well-being, and when they are diminished, so are we.

The Contribution of Christian Teachings

The Christian churches, including the Roman Catholic Church, have been the major architects and chief enforcers of compulsory heterosexual monogamy. Even though Jesus lived in a discipleship of equals with women and other subordinates in his society, hatred of women and hatred of sexuality have been "an active force profoundly deforming Christianity's own internal structure and ideology for centuries."[67] No connection between religion and sexual repression was inevitable or fated.

Christianity began in the first century as a revolutionary move-ment of women, slaves, and poor people who were joined by socially dominant allies. In the fourth century, Christianity became a power-ful state religion in service of elite interests. When the church capitu-lated to Constantine and supported the religion of empire, ordinary Christians had to discard their roles of opposing oppressive power relations, including opposition to Roman war-making. The emerging church leadership abandoned egalitarian models and adopted Roman hierarchy and the social relations of feudalism, thereby establishing a new identity for Christians.

Historical theologian Samuel Laeuchli dates the origin of the church's antisexual code to the Council of Elvira, Spain, in 309 C.E. Laeuchli explains, "By establishing sexual codes the synod meant to define the particular character of Christian life; by setting sexual ta-boos, the synod meant to create the image of an ascetic clerical lead-ership."[68] Living by restrictive sexual codes gave a new definition to being a Christian, as it also gave the hierarchy the role of enforcing these codes. Identifying the Council of Elvira as the starting point for the church's preoccupation with a repressive "pelvic theology," Catholic ethicist Daniel Maguire argues that regulated sexuality became the litmus test to define orthodoxy and the focus of church authority.[69]

Drawing on anti-body and erotophobic attitudes from classical antiquity, the Christian churches have been primary cultural conduits of hatred, fear, and ignorance about sexuality. The Catholic Church's sexual ethic is a highly regulated marriage ethic organized around child rearing and detailed in Pope Pius XI's 1930 encyclical, "On Christian Marriage" (*Casti Connubii*). The church's version of compulsory het-erosexual monogamy requires sacramental marriage and excludes birth control, abortion, sterilization, and divorce.[70] The marriage ethic re-quires women to be either a virgin or a properly married mother, and to follow the example of such saints as Maria Goretti, who chose death rather than rape. Catholic women have learned that without their in-tact hymens or multiple experiences of married motherhood, they have no right to exist. For men, church teaching reinforces male socializa-tion, especially the repression of emotions and desires. However, room is given men to believe that sexual desire is beyond their control. This belief is supported by traditional moral theology that defined birth control as more sinful than rape because with rape procreation, the only legitimate purpose of sexual desire, was at least possible.

This sexual teaching is foundational to many ills. It enslaves women and makes our very existence subservient to the condition or fruitfulness of our sexual and reproductive organs. By equating women with a (sinful) sexuality, this teaching denies our personhood and violates our bodyright. It gives men implicit permission for sexual violence as it outlaws most sexual expression. It has been a chief ally to industrial morality and racist, capitalist managerial control.

Perhaps worst of all, this sex-negative legacy leads Christians to believe that our bodies are alien forces. The marriage ethic teaches that sexual desire is highly suspect, an enemy of the true self that is at war with spiritual well-being. The history of Christian asceticism shows how pain, especially the deprivation of sensual pleasure, is viewed as the foundation for the moral and spiritual life. Christianity becomes a handmaiden of the exploitative and oppressive status quo as it conditions people to desire pain, subordination, and powerlessness and to fear pleasure, self-assertion, and personal power.[71]

The scandal of this tradition has been acknowledged in recent decades by many Catholic ethicists. Certainly, Daniel Maguire has long been a critic of obsessive pelvic theology. Moral theologian Margaret A. Farley observes that "nearly every traditional moral rule governing sexual behavior in Western culture is today being challenged."[72] Ethicist Barbara Hilkert Andolsen found an examination of "my church's moral memories" to be "profoundly alienating." Andolsen says that "the materials concerning sexuality usually encompassed by the phrase 'the Roman Catholic tradition' are a painful and sometimes repulsive collection."[73] Christine Gudorf looks to more hopeful signs in the Dutch Reformed Church's public repentance for its teaching on apartheid, and the repentance of the Catholic Church at Vatican II for its historic anti-Semitism. Gudorf contends that "the same kind of renunciation of traditional teaching in sexuality, followed by repentance, is necessary on the part of all Christian churches today in response to the suffering and victimization it has long supported and legitimated."[74] There is great need for churches to affirm an ethical eroticism that supports desire and pleasure as essential for human well-being and personal empowerment. One immediate task is to sketch some general outlines of such an ethic, and then as Catholic ethicist Mary Hunt suggests, the churches should "leave the rest up to the good sense of faithful people to be self-directive in these matters."[75]

Sketching an Ethical Eroticism

An ethical eroticism would support our need, as social beings, to connect sensually with ourselves, with the natural world, with human work, and with the many others with whom we share passionate interdependence.

An ethical eroticism would transform our relations to ourselves. It would recognize that we, like all living systems, evolve in variety and resilience the more we are open to our environment. Joanna Macy and Molly Brown remind us that we are beings who do not have armor for exterior covering, but soft and sensitive skin, lips, tongues, ears, eyes, fingertips, and genitals, all of which enable communication and interaction with our environment. Severe regulation of our communicative capacities through power-over dynamics is dysfunctional because it prevents feedback and diversity. Such regulation prevents our growth and well-being as relational selves able to engage in moral reflection and self-critical evaluation. Our capacity to respond to our environment with passion and compassion, if unblocked, will flow forth from our profound mutuality.[76] An ethical eroticism would nurture passion and its progeny compassion instead of fearing, loathing, and regulating it.

Because we are embodied beings, an ethical eroticism would respect the gifts that the body, and only the body, can give to the spirit. As infants, we would not have survived had we not been surrounded by loving, careful touching and caressing from other human beings. No matter how well fed, an infant will not survive, let alone flourish, without warmth, comfort, and continual flesh-to-flesh contact with other human bodies.

Many people mistakenly believe we leave the need for touch behind in childhood. Our increasing divorce from the natural world, the alienating nature of the capitalist workplace, the racist coding of sexual desire, and the restrictions of heterosexual monogamy leave little opportunity for sensuous human contact in most areas of our lives. As seen in the anthropological research discussed in this chapter, many societies would evaluate ours as one in which most people are starved for touch and pleasure deprived. An ethical eroticism would value nurturing touch, including but by no means exhausted by mutual sexual pleasuring. Nurturing touch is a major resource for the energy needed to make peace and justice.

An ethical eroticism would support our learning about, experimenting with, and developing a symbolic and physical language about our bodies as sources of communication, nurturant interaction, and passionate expression. It would help us think about coitus as only one possibility (and often not the best possibility) among sexual options. Psychologist Sandra Lipsitz Bem has redefined sex as "an open-ended interaction that needs to be custom choreographed by every new set of participants."[77] Such sexuality requires leisure, permission for experimentation, trust in our bodies, and belief in our right to pleasure. However, all these claims are repugnant to an erotophobic workaholic culture that makes people believe they deserve subordination and pain.

When patriarchal, racist, capitalist culture uses and abuses bodies for its vested interests, it teaches people to distrust their bodies. As a result, even dominants are shut off from themselves, suffer deep distortions of the body's wisdom, and are alienated from personal power. An ethical eroticism would challenge this situation and trust in our ability to critically evaluate it.

For example, an ethical eroticism would respond differently from the authorities in my child's day care center years ago. Impelled by a widely publicized trial of a center operator who was accused of sexually molesting children in her care, the director of my child's center prohibited the caregivers from holding the children on their laps during story time or giving the children back rubs before naps. This touch deprivation was very hard on both the adults and the children. The employees were no longer the "aunts and uncles" from whom the children expected physical nurturance at the center and during their visits to the home. Because touching in our culture is too often violent and life-threatening, it takes courage to insist that we need *more* nurturant touching, not less. I agree with theologian Mary Pellauer, who encourages us to "talk at length about the gifts the body gives to the spirit."[78]

The human body is not the only source of spiritual gifts. Even the most expansive sexual experiences will not fully satisfy human erotic needs. As beings who emerged from the amniotic waters of the sea, we need visceral experiences of water, earth, air, sky, forest, mountains, and other earth creatures for emotional balance and for a sense of basic well-being. In contrast to the violent touching of plunder and exploitation, an ethical eroticism would transform our relationship to the natural world to that of nurture, listening, sensuous interaction, and respectful interdependence. An ethical eroticism rejects abusing the earth as supply house and sewer; it recognizes that earth, air, and water flow through our veins and organs, and that we are body extensions of our mother the earth. When she is healthy, so are we, and when she is diseased, we suffer and die prematurely. We need close, harmonious interaction with the earth not only to sustain our bodies but also to maintain emotional and spiritual equilibrium. An ethical eroticism challenges overconsumption, capitalism's life root of profit making that requires massive ecological abuse and destruction.

An ethical eroticism would challenge the work ethic and the capitalist workplace. Under current arrangements, most bodies at work are divorced from their erotic needs and become appendages of machines. Human instruments of profit making must be numbed to their desire for communion with others in order to sustain nonsensuous, nongratifying, isolating labor. An ethical eroticism would challenge this situation. It would support democratic control over work, including what is made, the process by which it is made, the resources used, and where the profits go. An ethical eroticism would make work a source of gratification in and of itself, as people do socially useful, self-gratifying, sensuous labor together.

An ethical eroticism will also be resisted because it challenges dominant/subordinate relations and puts them into crisis. An ethical eroticism challenges heterogender and the formation of truncated human beings. It challenges the reproduction of women as an unpaid and underpaid laboring class. Even as the waste from capitalist abundance suffocates the planet, an ethical eroticism challenges the ubiquitous belief that we must live in an economy of scarcity—in jobs, education, health care, and love. An ethical eroticism challenges racism and the identification of shared sexual power with lewdness and promiscuity. It challenges submissiveness and conformity because people in touch with their desire are less likely to tolerate victimization of themselves or others.

An ethical eroticism expands the erotic to include far more than the sexual, and it expands the sexual to include more than hetero-gendered, male-focused orgasm. An ethical eroticism enlarges the stunted roles for loving that the culture requires of us. It affirms the material world and teaches that our very survival depends on listening to the wisdom of our bodies and the ecosphere. It affirms our reality as species-beings who are interdependent on other bodies and rely on passionate, sensuous, mutual, and self-critical interactions for our well-being.

An ethical eroticism challenges the dangerous homogenization in nature and culture. *It affirms the goodness of a variety of life-forms in the human and natural worlds, including the multiple ways people need to express ourselves as sexed, gendered, sexual, and erotic beings.* It honors multiple relationships of varying emotional intensity. It makes space for rich, lifelong egalitarian partnerships, especially those that renegotiate the terms of fidelity according to the evolving friendship and intimacy needs of the partners. It affirms radically reconstructed work where sensuous interdependent beings spend most of their lives, often in antiseptic environments and alienated isolation.

Finally, an ethical eroticism helps us be forgiving when we make mistakes. It anticipates that we will make errors of judgment, perhaps even be driven by jealousy and pettiness. It trusts our capacity to be self-critical as we slowly work our way out of nonmutual, abusive, and possessive ways of interacting. This trust is grounded in the belief that as species-beings in profound interdependence for our survival and flourishing, compassion is possible for us. An ethical eroticism knows that unearthing this treasure will take conflict, resistance, risk taking, and courage. Though often blocked by our sex/gender system and the vested interests it promotes, compassion, essential to our survival as interdependent beings, is a possibility that flows through us all.

5

Relational Labor and the Politics of Solidarity

> Relationships . . . are the essence of life and morality.
> —Anthony Cortese

As we have seen throughout the previous chapters, systems of privilege and oppression divide people into groups so that social, political, and economic power remains unshared. Dominant groups monopolize privileged access to the benefits of the society. Subordinate groups bear a disproportionate share of society's burdens. The privileged are also in charge of knowledge making and create an all-pervasive ideology that justifies this set of arrangements as "commonsense" in the everyday workings of the society. *At the same time, however, dominant groups share a common vulnerability because they depend on the labor and caretaking roles of subordinates as well as the rapidly diminishing resources of the biosphere.* It is also true, as this analysis has shown, that people in privileged positions are shrinking in numbers as maleness, whiteness, and class location protect fewer people from the harsh fallout of the restructured global economy.

Given this situation, elites who take Christian vocation seriously have much to do in building a moral world. As previous chapters have argued, we need to understand the dimensions of unshared class, race, and gender power so that we can intervene in our lives and resist reproducing unjust social relations. The difficulty of this task is intensified by the ambiguity and complexity of our moral agency. We find claiming our power for social transformation difficult because we occupy multiple social locations, live in relative isolation from other groups, and are overexposed to the logic of current arrangements through elite forms of education.

Even so, we can learn much from dominant groups. The most powerful elites maintain and increase their power by being super-organized within their groups. As has been noted, the economic, political, and cultural power enjoyed by elites enables them to exercise disproportionate influence in such sectors as business, government, academia, media, and religion. Through these institutions, the most privileged define the vested interests, cultural values, and social behaviors imposed on others.

If justice is to increase, the majority who occupy positions of subordination, including many of the elites addressed here, must become as organized as the most powerful. Subordinates, however, remain largely divided even when they organize to increase their power. Focused primarily on their individually subordinate identities, groups representing low-income people, communities of color, white women, and gays and lesbians, for example, often remain separated and isolated from other subordinate groups.

Philosopher Janet Jakobsen argues that the potential challenge to the status quo represented by these groups is largely contained as each group focuses only on those with power at the center. White women, low-income people, people of color, and gay people often ignore one another while struggling to become more like the norm—white, affluent, heterosexual, and male. Each group, says Jakobsen, becomes co-opted and "trapped in difference" when it advocates for its interests within the terms and norms set by dominants.[1]

Why Diverse Subordinates Are Natural Allies

A primary way the most powerful keep subordinate groups from relating to one another is by making them appear homogeneous and distinct when, in fact, they are heterogeneous and overlapping. For example, some may analyze how women are deeply divided among themselves without noting how their internal divisions unite them with other groups. Recognizing the *diversity within* groups can become the basis for discerning the *commonality among* groups.[2] For example, many women share common cause with men who occupy similar subordinate positions in the systems of class, race, and sexuality. This means that women as a group benefit when we recognize our commonalities with working-class men who are also treated as bodies to be used for profits by dominants. Those concerned with gender oppression, therefore, benefit from those working against class exploitation. Low-income groups are natural allies to feminists whenever they challenge the economic superexploitation of women who do not have the freedom to choose to live independently from abusive partners or employers.

Groups concerned about class exploitation and the well-being of poor and low-income people need feminist groups when they understand how gender oppression is a basis for class elitism. Deeply ingrained in the social world of children, the gender-polarized and heteronormative family teaches them that dominant/subordinate relations everywhere in the society are normal and natural. In addition, the exploitation of women as a sex class in the home and the labor market is essential for capitalist profit making and the reproduction of class society. Exploitative class relations are deeply intertwined with abusive gender relations and could not exist without them.

Groups concerned with the racial system benefit from the struggle of low-income groups and those addressing sexual oppression. Groups concerned with racial oppression need alliances with low-income groups because diverse communities of color continue to overserve the economy by being forced into a disproportionate share of the most dangerous and exploited labor as well as the highest amounts of underemployment and unemployment. People of color also benefit from the efforts of gay liberation groups who share common oppression from a sexual system that requires scapegoats to carry the rejected erotic self fundamental to achieving racially and sexually normative status in this culture.

Similarly, those concerned with gay oppression need to dismantle the class, race, and gender systems. This is particularly evident when we realize that the vast majority of homosexuals in the world are working-class women of color.[3] In addition, most whites would benefit from acknowledging their shared interest with nonwhites who are also exploited by the class system and/or oppressed by the sex/gender system. Groups working for ecological justice need to understand that there will be no care for the planet as long as the economic system makes all things into commodities in the service of profits for shareholders. Groups working for environmental justice need to see that capitalist development, ecological degradation, and increasing poverty are different aspects of the same problem.[4] Groups working for environmental justice need feminist, antiracist, and gay liberation groups as well. There will also be no real caring for the planet itself as long as the sexual system requires the regulation and abuse of everyone and everything associated with the sensual material world and the negative erotic. To work for the environment is to work to transform all social and material relations.

Understanding how these systems feed off and reinforce one another (even as they sometimes work at cross-purposes) makes it evident that there will be no economic justice, gender justice, racial justice, sexual justice, or ecological justice until there is justice for all. Nicola Field observes, "Our most important task is to show how oppressions affect everyone because they divide us . . . [and they] all come from the same system."[5]

When identity groups realize the benefits each will receive from a collective effort to challenge the common system affecting us all, we increase the possibilities for social movements that challenge unshared power.[6] Consequently, ethics, as Jakobsen explores it, involves first and foremost the "relational labor" or "moral labor" of working out alliances among social groups.[7] These alliances take advantage of the possibilities for relationship at the intersections of class, race, gender, and sexuality systems. Alliances use diversity *within* groups to make connections *between* subordinate groups, so that new political action can occur with a larger critical mass who share common concerns. Increased challenge to the status quo becomes possible as the marginalized forge complex relationships among their groups.[8]

From this paradigm, moral agency is primarily activated not by the individual who exercises "free choice," but by groups involved in the relational labor of creating new forms of social relationships that, in turn, can build new social movements. Building "solidarity across differences," mobilizing differences to challenge our assigned roles as dominants and subordinates and to interrupt the unshared power of dominant groups at various sites of privilege/oppression, is the major site of moral agency.[9]

Why Alliances Are Hard to Build

Alliances are hard to build for many reasons. Most erotically disempowered people are socialized to be passive consumers of what organizations have to offer rather than builders of new, democratically participatory institutions. In addition, major theoretical constructs, such as postmodernism, condition us to accept the fragmentation and isolation surrounding us. Some see postmodernism as a form of capitalist crisis management because it teaches us to confine resistance and struggle to regional and isolated sites and to reject all master narratives.[10] Alliances, however, are the only ways to build the critical mass needed to create practices of resistance in order to address the master interlocking system of male-dominant, racist capitalism that works against most people's real interests.

Alliances are also hard to build because the Religious Right has been working arduously over the past decade to increase the divide along the separations that alliances need to overcome. Using racism in white communities, sexism in gay communities, and homophobia in communities of color, the Right has been successful in organizing masses of ordinary people by increasing fear among voters so they will roll back civil rights and social services that benefit everyone. Educator and activist Susan Pharr observes that "while the Right is united by their racism, sexism and homophobia in their goal to dominate all of us, we are divided by our own racism, sexism and homophobia—and divided we are falling. . . . We have to understand that if any one group can be left out, then reasons can be found to leave any other group out."[11]

Here it is evident that alliances are hard to build because many people need enemies upon which to project those nonnormative parts of themselves that must be rejected in order to maintain the present disorder. As has been discussed, surviving the systems of male-dominant, racist, class-stratified society requires most people, and perhaps especially the privileged, to reject our vulnerability, spontaneity, and sensuality. As we suffer, we often feel a need to punish and control others. We also expect them to put up with their own pain and suffering. Only when we can generate compassion for our own bodily needs, vulnerability, and dependence upon others will we experience the compassion for others that is necessary for solidarity work. Only when those in privileged groups perceive exactly how *even we deserve better* will we be released from our need to punish and control others, so we can form alliances with them.

The need for external enemies, and the related assumption that our agenda has no moral ambiguity, is probably the major obstacle to alliance formation. Alliances help groups acknowledge that the enemy resides not only without, but also within us and the collectives we forge because all the dominant/subordinate dynamics of society are present within the alliance itself. As much as alliance formation requires self- and group affirmation in a society that demands self-negation from most, alliances also require humility. Alliances will not happen if affluent males do not control their propensity to take over, or if white women do not challenge our desire to run from conflict. Similarly, just as the enemy is within, so the ally may be without. In gaining recognition that we are deeply flawed, we may gain recognition that our enemy may be capable of wisdom and insight. Living ethically means becoming alert to our own self-righteousness as well as giving credit to the opposition's capacity for compassion.

Jakobsen and Pharr agree that we must go beyond the notion that diversity is a threat to effective action. In fact, Jakobsen contends, alliances of diverse constituencies are the *only* means to challenge dominant culture and its rigidity, conformity, and unshared power arrangements. As long as subordinates and their potential allies from dominant groups remain isolated in their differences, they pose no threat to the status quo. *What is a threat is not difference but similarity in cause.* When diverse subordinates and their dominant allies discover common cause together, the status quo will not continue. Allies may and do disagree, they do not have a common identity, and they may lack a single normative framework. However, when they understand common concerns, sorrows, and joys as the real connections among them, *they can work together to interrupt exploitation and oppression even if disagreements remain.*[12]

Common cause, then, does not require sameness. As has been discussed, discovering common cause includes discovering how homogenizing trends in nature and culture are dangerous to all. Alliances focus not on creating similarity, but on challenging the norms and behaviors that support the privileges of dominant groups and maintain the systems of unshared power that hurt most. As complex networks constructed in and between differences, alliances cross borders in search of practical solidarity even as each group within the alliance maintains its particular claims.[13]

However powerful the social forces working against solidarity, major thinkers of this century credit less-powerful groups with the ability to think and act creatively for their well-being and flourishing. Theorists such as Italian Marxist Antonio Gramsci and Frankfurt School theorist Jürgen Habermas recognize the enormous power of the status quo to shape people into conformity and consensus. Given the experiences of fascism, Soviet dictatorship, and American mass culture, it would have been easy for them to be pessimistic about social emancipation. Nevertheless, they insisted that while people are socially constructed, they are also capable of critical evaluation and intervention in the social world. For Habermas, communicating subjects are capable of creative accomplishments independent of the social forces directing the society.[14]

Gramsci also focused on ideological and cultural factors in bringing about social change, stressing the counterhegemonic (or subordinate) knowledge found in ethical frameworks and religious views at the margins of society. He believed that a massive collective movement could achieve hegemonic status if it emerged from grassroots democratic energy rooted in local traditions and willing to engage in long-term struggle.[15] Theorists such as these support the possibility of a democratic reconstruction of society through the communicative interaction of "unruly subjects" in coalition politics.[16]

Despite all the difficulties working against solidarity, alliances need to happen. No matter our degree of vulnerability, everyone's "distance from economic necessity is dwindling."[17] According to Jakobsen, the work of alliance formation is never finished, but remains "constitutive of on-going moral and political life."[18] This relational labor, as labor activist Kim Moody describes, increases our understanding of society, hones our collaborative skills, and expands the sense of the possible.[19]

Relational Labor and the Prophetic Imagination

The possibility for solidarity also finds support in religious tradition, which further illuminates the relational labor necessary for solidarity work. One such tradition is what Scripture scholar Walter Brueggemann calls "the prophetic imagination." The work of the Hebrew prophets, as well as the ministry of Jesus, brought people together to identify their suffering and engage their longing for social transformation. The prophet engages in the work of grieving and refusing to deny or numb oneself to the suffering in the society. When people grieve together, they challenge the notion that feeling pain for the world is only a matter of personal maladjustment. When people grieve, they challenge society's propensity to cover up structures of privilege and oppression, violence and death. The prophet unveils "the barriers and pecking orders that secure us at each other's expense, and the fearful practice of eating off the table of a hungry brother and sister."[20] The prophets who weep and mourn call people out of their apathy, numbness, and isolation, all of which are essential to protect unshared power arrangements and maintain the enormous suffering of the status quo. Without numbness to protect them from their own and others' suffering, people begin to see their interdependence, face their vulnerabilities, identify the common roots of their suffering, and enter into a grieving process. Like the work of Amos and Jeremiah before him, Jesus' work of solidarity involved weeping over the self-deception of Jerusalem and claiming that only those who mourned would find comfort.[21]

The comfort brought about by the prophetic work of grieving is the result of coming to terms with one's loss by acknowledging a vision of life that has yet to be realized. Grieving is "the public expression of those very hopes and yearnings that have been denied so long and suppressed so deeply that we no longer know they are there."[22]

In recent decades many people in the United States have lamented what is perceived to be a widespread loss of concern for public affairs and for the common good among the citizenry. Certainly, the preoccupation by the affluent with individual gain in the marketplace, as well as the preoccupation of those losing economic ground with the very survival of their families, is on the rise. Many in Congress seem to believe that people's preoccupations with individual issues is such that politicians can govern without taking into account voters' concerns. Former senator Alan Simpson from Wyoming reflects this view when he says that what citizens think is expendable to people in government because "the attention span of Americans is which movie is coming out next month and whether the quarterly report on their stock will change."[23] While Simpson is certainly correct that voters tend to be those who own stocks, not all would agree that preoccupation with oneself and one's family is the last word.

It is certainly not so for the Religious Right, which has enlisted hundreds of thousands to promote the antidemocratic agenda that Suzanne Pharr noted above. As a response to the political apathy that followed Vietnam and Watergate, the superorganized Religious Right moved into the vacuum and infiltrated all levels of politics. By the early 1990s there were 48 state units of the Christian Coalition with 17,000 neighborhood coordinators, 30,000 local workers, and contacts in 60,000 churches. Since no one else is organized to this degree, the Religious Right has been able to wage a politics of hate with between 17 and 34 percent of the electorate.[24] Those of us interested in a politics of compassion have much to learn from the organizational strategies of the Right.

However, 17 to 34 percent of the electorate does not a majority make. Many people still experience the need for the kind of compassion affirmed in classical antiquity, the Catholic tradition, feminist theory, and the work of Marxists such as Gramsci and critical theorists such as Habermas. Sociologist Richard Sennett is among those who demonstrate hope about the human person as fundamentally a self-in-relation with a compassionate potential. Among the workers he recently studied in various American cities, Sennett witnessed indifference and a lack of interest in civic affairs, but also outrage at the lack of commitment, accountability, and responsibility in contemporary life. Sennett believes that "one of the unintended consequences of modern capitalism is that it has strengthened the value of place, aroused a longing for community . . . for some other scene of attachment and depth."[25] This longing is also demonstrated by the reservoir of resistance to the current political climate being played out at the international, national, and community levels in such places as the evolving AFL-CIO and the growing number of grassroots organizations across the United States and in the Two-Thirds World.[26]

Grounds for hope persist insofar as people are capable of acknowledging loss, capturing a vision of life that is yet to be realized, and displaying the power of ordinary people to develop practices that resist the relations of rule. The biblical prophets are relevant here in that they remind us that a certain comfort comes from publicly mourning "against permanent consignment to chaos, oppression, barrenness and exile."[27] This comfort is a gift that comes only with "decisive solidarity with marginal people and the accompanying vulnerability required by that solidarity."[28]

The prophetic imagination brings comfort because in their solidarity and shared vulnerability with suffering people, those who mourn can uncover the violation and human pain that dominant groups must deny to remain in power. The work of solidarity brings comfort because it insists that much social suffering is not normal or natural, it challenges all norms and behaviors that support unshared power, and it struggles for a community where there are no excluded ones. Brueggemann argues that because of Jesus' solidarity with poor and marginalized people, and because of his conflict with the powers that be, he was able to birth an alternative consciousness and stake out possibilities for a new age, a new social order.[29]

In his insistence on compassion and solidarity as the foundation of social relations, Jesus promoted not liberal do-goodism, but harsh criticism and a radical threat to the structures and worldviews that promote and justify suffering.[30] Groups who monopolize power can tolerate charity, but they cannot survive masses of exploited and oppressed people, as well as their allies, standing in solidarity with one another as they resist structures of violence.[31] *Precisely because it will no longer tolerate unnoticed pain, the work of solidarity signals a social revolution.* Only when suffering is identified, and resisted, is the status quo discredited and transformation made possible.

Where is the hope for people with elite privilege? Only when we can grieve about the fact that in order to maintain our lifestyles we cannot have full access to ourselves and to the friendship of others can we begin to move forward. *Only when we can grieve about the cultural, political, economic, and sexual structures that deeply distort our own potential as human beings can we move forward.* Only in the process of mourning and sharing the pain with others will we be able to unearth the loving connections that still remain possible in the emotional underground of this society. Making these connections is essential to the work of solidarity and social transformation.

Relational Labor and Christian Ethics

In a similar vein, Christian ethicist Ada María Isasi-Díaz suggests that solidarity through alliance building is the new name for genuine love of the neighbor. Alliance building is a discernment of mutuality and a practice of lifelong political struggle. When we work to discern the structures that alienate us from one another, as this book tries to do, we come to understand how justice making benefits everyone. People in dominant groups can become "friends" to subordinates, and together they can form alliances that enable all to see that vengeance is not the goal of the struggle, but the achievement of solidarity. Through alliances, subordinates and the privileged can change their history so that the entire "Kindom" of God can flourish together. As Isasi-Díaz affirms, new structures supportive of liberation are a historical possibility; allies must create them together in lifelong political action.[32]

The work of solidarity, therefore, is not only the work of forging new alliances among subordinates. It also involves the relational labor of forging dominant-subordinate alliances. If the creation of a more just society depends upon expanding the arena of democratic struggle across class, race, gender, and sexuality lines, this will happen only when the privileged can grieve about our own losses and become clearer about how solidarity benefits us as well. The work of solidarity can be embraced by elites who know we are damaged by present arrangements and realize what is at stake for us in collective action for social transformation.

Even so, relational labor remains hard work for everyone. Finding ways to challenge our assigned positions as dominants and subordinates and to resist hierarchical power arrangements often seems an impossibility. For we live in a world where people are giving up what power they have all the time as corporate, religious, and cultural authorities consolidate control over an increasingly homogenized society. Dualistic thinking also inhibits us when we are tempted to believe that some people monopolize virtue and others monopolize vice. We think that if we can identify and challenge the opposition, there will be certitude on the road to a just society.

In her provocative study about the struggle to achieve alliances, ethicist Sharon Welch offers jazz as an important model for thinking and strategizing about solidarity. Welch is especially interested in jazz because this African American art form can help us remain aware of the moral ambiguity that always accompanies struggles for justice.

Drawing extensively from her political work, Welch shows how dualistic ways of thinking can be deadly to the creation of mutuality and accountability in relationships. Jazz is a significant counterpoint here because this musical tradition defies dualistic ways of being in the world (us against them, joy versus sorrow, the moral versus the immoral). Jazz is a model of relational labor since it "emerges from the interplay of structure and improvisation, collectivity and individuality, tradition and innovation." Jazz gives clues about the positive power of grieving as it holds together pathos and joy and refuses to accept societal limits. Jazz is full of risk taking; it is open ended and never completed. Jazz is serious but always ready to laugh at itself. Jazz is intensely mutual and not afraid of failure. Some of the best jazz has to do with *improvisations on people's mistakes.* "The worst thing that can be said of a jazz player," says Welch, "is that he or she doesn't listen."[33]

Welch finds jazz a helpful model for justice seekers in order to open us to risks and to the fact that we are as capable of deep moral failure as our opposition is capable of compassion and justice. Jazz is attuned to the fact that there are no guaranteed outcomes, and that we can deepen relationships with one another by working through conflicts. *Jazz is a helpful model for justice seekers when it most values the integrity of the process as well as the outcome.* What is most important and moral is not our agenda or goals. Of most value is the struggle to achieve balanced relationships and to acknowledge our interdependence as we grow in accountability to one another. *For Welch, solidarity and compassion are possible not because they are ethically mandated, but because they bring human beings so much joy.*[34]

In a talk about his work to close the U.S. School of the Americas, which trains Latin American military in torture and assassination methods against the resisting poor, Father Roy Bourgeois exemplifies the values articulated in Welch's notion of relational labor. Bourgeois tells how he and his companions in the School of the Americas Watch dress up in army fatigues, bearing the names of those tortured and disappeared on their lapels. In Charlie Chaplin style, they dutifully practice the military salute. Sneaking into the school's courtyard, they plant a boom box in a tree opposite the dormitory where the soldiers-in-training have retired for the night. The boom box blares out Bishop Oscar Romero's last sermon before his assassination at the hands of the School's graduates. In the sermon Romero pleads with the military to "stop the killing" of the multitudes of poor who resist exploitation and oppression.

Bourgeois and the other resisters end up in prison, of course, with the harshest possible sentence meted out by a southern segregationist judge they affectionately call "Maximum Bob." When the judge gives them a minute to speak at the end of the sentencing, Bourgeois and his companions invite the judge to join them in their next protest, which the judge has guaranteed they will have plenty of time to plan carefully while in prison.

Such playful but serious resistance, which refuses to honor the dualisms rampant in the culture, entices people to join such movements and use their own dramatic energy to imagine creative change. The numbers keeping vigil outside the School have grown significantly over the last few years. When the most recent resolution to close the School came up before Congress, the vote was only eleven votes shy of passing in a Republican-controlled Congress.[35]

As we better understand the construction of social relations and the process of creative, nondualistic relational labor, we can see how liberal individualism and Christian altruism are inadequate guides to our social reality and moral agency. A moral analysis of current arrangements and an understanding of the ethics of relational labor are necessary to move into broad-based coalitions and solidarity work.

Analysis Is Not Politics

For genuine solidarity to become a reality, social analysis alone is not sufficient. As previously argued, the energy to imagine and seek a new future can come only through grief work and collective resistance, both foundational for a politics of compassion and solidarity. Indeed, people can be morally and emotionally disgusted with what the system is doing, but still cooperate because they see no alternative. To address the massive monopolization of power and the steadfast erosion of securities, securities that a just society would confer on everyone, we must be willing to experiment with a new future and move through analysis to the politics of solidarity work. Building on the work of such ethicists and activists as those cited in this chapter, we need to develop strategies for alliance building and for developing a comprehensive array of pragmatic actions that can work in everyday life to energize us for further struggles to increase power sharing. [36]

Those who write books also need to log in our hours in the struggle to build alliances. We must join or create constituencies in addition to our academic audiences. Educator Henry Giroux writes that we need to specify "the leaky and contradictory nature of dominant power," we need to "reframe the debates," we need to move into "the spaces of resistance within dominant forums," and we must "hijack such sites as talk radio."[37] We must learn from the Religious Right and their superior organizational ability, even as we use such models as jazz to critique their deep dualism and our self-righteousness. We must identify, resist, and transform the relations of unshared power that promote class stratification, racism, sexism, and other oppressive conditions. We need to study the creative, nondualistic movements already in process and play more jazz with one another.

To maintain integrity and faithfulness, the churches themselves must be part of the politics of solidarity and alliance formation. Theologian Delores Williams says that when the church ignores economic, racial, sexual, and other forms of violence and abuse of power, "it forfeits its right to be identified as the church of Jesus Christ." Williams asserts that "without a viable commitment to help stop the violence whites do to blacks, men do to women, economically powerful people do to poor people, the Christian church loses its marks of apostolicity, catholicity, unity and holiness."[38] Here is indeed a challenge for Christian institutions that too often promote the hierarchical status quo. Churches must also be transformed in order to create spaces and opportunities for us to analyze, grieve, imagine, be playful, strategize, and not become discouraged when our mistakes are large. We know that privileged people, even privileged churches, are capable of changing our theory and our politics. If we are to survive, we must be able to grieve and mourn the ignorance, arrogance, isolation, and destruction spawned by lives based on unearned advantages. Elites must mourn the pseudovalues and impoverished social relations that define most aspects of our privileged lives. We must grieve the loss of our integrity and the threat to the very survival of the planet itself that is posed by current arrangements. Only then will we be able to change the way we see ourselves and our religious traditions, the way we view others, and the way we behave. We must understand that solidarity and new alliances forged within concrete projects for social change are not a utopian dream. Rather, solidarity is the extension of our fundamental interdependence, as inherently social beings, as members of the one body of Christ, and, yes, as persons who collectively are increasingly subordinate to our market value in generating profits.

Perhaps most important of all, solidarity and alliance building provide the means for us to recover our fundamental humanity. Our very humanity is at stake when we see how profoundly damaged we are by internalized superiority and by systems that exploit and oppress most of the people on the globe today. When we no longer deny the environmental destruction that threatens us all, we know that nothing less than fundamental social change will give even the privileged a future.

The Nature of Authentic Privilege

To strengthen solidarity, we can draw on dangerous historical memories as well as on current examples, which show the capacities of human beings to defy social hierarchies and care for one another and the earth. We are not only people who benefit from white unearned advantage; we also fight police brutality, economic exploitation, redlining, unequal access to education and health care, and the toxic waste of current production. We are not only practicing heterosexuals, but supporters of gay, lesbian, bisexual, and transgendered persons and their rights, we resist ownership patterns in our own intimate relations, and we do not assume that our children are straight. We are not only privileged men; we also scrub toilets, nurture children, educate about male violence, and challenge hierarchy at home, at work, in politics, and in the churches. We are not only economi-

cally affluent; we work for clean elections, progressive taxes to ⌣
port the common good, unions, and welfare rights, and we oppose
the global system of war making. We are not only affluent white
women, but we are allies of women of color and of lower working
class/poor women of all races.

This work of fighting for a better life continues in large and small
ways in local communities and throughout the globe. We need to
find these experiments in freedom, extend them, and create more of
them. Elites need to decide the groups or communities to which we
will be accountable with our limited social power and financial resources. Even as we take baby steps, we change and grow and become
capable of bigger steps.

We have considered a variety of religious, ethical, and intellectual
traditions that analyze our privilege and mounting peril for all, affirm
a politics of compassion, and challenge us to work out the necessary
strategies needed to arrive there. Some suggest that the more complex
solidarity becomes, and the more sectors of the population are drawn
into it, the more clearly will the present disorder become apparent. As
a consequence, more alternatives to the status quo, largely invisible
to us now, will emerge as possibilities. The very process of grieving
and resisting in new spaces, constructed in and between differences,
will generate hope.

Others caution that profound change is possible only if we remain wary of dualisms that contaminate even our best analyses, strategies, and goals. The challenge includes living more humbly, carefully—and playfully—in the midst of moral ambiguity and, yes, even
failure. This requires focusing our primary energies not only on outcomes, but on the quality of relationships we can build and enjoy
along the way. As Elisabeth Schüssler Fiorenza has commented similarly about the earliest Christians, the journey is more to the point
even than the goal.

To begin, we need to be wherever people are "fighting for a better
life—no matter how basic that fight might seem."[39] The late Sr. Marjorie
Tuite, educator and activist for people in the margins, once announced:
"I am working for a world I will never see. But it is a privilege to be
part of the struggle." The privilege that elites must embrace is the privilege belonging to solidarity struggle. If we are to have a future on the
planet, this work must become our own.

*[" = books to
order! :)*

Notes

1. An Ethical Agenda for Elites

1. David Harvey, *Justice, Nature, and the Geography of Difference* (Cambridge, Mass.: Blackwell Publishers, 1996), 334–38.

2. Council on International and Public Affairs, "Why Today's Big Profits Mean Big Trouble," *Too Much*, fall 1995, 1.

3. Peggy McIntosh, "White Privilege and Male Privilege: A Personal Account of Coming to See Correspondences through Work in Women's Studies," working paper 189, Wellesley College Center for Research on Women, Wellesley, Mass., 1988.

4. Even though I reject the opposition in postmodernism to critical theories of class exploitation, racism, and gender subordination, as well as postmodernism's indifference to institutional change and social transformation, I follow its logic here in asserting that class, race, and gender differences are not essential but are social constructions. See Stephen Best and Douglas Kellner, *Postmodern Theory: Critical Interrogations* (New York: Guilford Press, 1991).

5. Patricia Hill Collins, *Fighting Words: Black Women and the Search for Justice* (Minneapolis: University of Minnesota Press, 1998), 102–3.

6. Lawrence Mishel, Jared Bernstein, and John Schmitt, *The State of Working America, 1998–1999* (Ithaca, N.Y.: Cornell University Press, 1999), 256–58.

7. Michael Parenti, *Power and the Powerless* (New York: St. Martin's Press, 1978), 11.

8. Mishel et al., *The State of Working America*, 51.

9. Parenti, *Power and the Powerless*, 12.

10. Himani Bannerji first used the word "commonsense" to denote the ubiquitous taken for granted assumptions undergirding racism. See Himani Bannerji, *Thinking Through: Essays on Feminism, Marxism, and Anti-Racism* (Toronto: Women's Press, 1995).

11. Francis Fox Piven and Richard A. Cloward, "Eras of Power," *Monthly Review*, January 1998, 11–23.

12. Parenti, *Power and the Powerless*, 5.

13. Michael Albert and Robin Hahnel, *Unorthodox Marxism: An Essay on Capitalism, Socialism, and Revolution* (Boston: South End Press, 1978), 61.

14. Parenti, *Power and the Powerless*, 13, 223.

154

15. Antonio Gramsci, *Selections from the Prison Notebooks of Antonio Gramsci*, ed. and trans. Quinton Hoare and Geoffrey Nowell Smith (New York: International Publishers, 1972).

16. Colin Nickerson, "Canadian Executive Returns as Hero from Colombia Ordeal," *Boston Globe*, 13 January 1999, sec. A.

17. Beverly W. Harrison, "The Fate of the Middle 'Class' in Late Capitalism," in *God and Capitalism: A Prophetic Critique of Market Economy*, ed. J. Mark Thomas and Vernon Visick (Madison, Wisc.: A-R Editions, 1991), 55.

18. Bannerji, "But Who Will Speak for Us?" in *Unsettling Relations*, ed. Himani Bannerji et al. (Boston: South End Press, 1991), 84.

19. Critical theory in a narrow sense refers to the intellectual tradition established by the Frankfurt School for Social Research in 1923 and includes the more recent work of Jürgen Habermas. While I draw on some of these theorists, I use a broader definition of critical social theory that draws on bodies of knowledge that actively engage the central issues facing groups who live in contexts characterized by class, race, and gender injustice. See David Held, *Introduction to Critical Theory: Horkheimer to Habermas* (Berkeley: University of California Press, 1980), and Collins, *Fighting Words*, 124–54.

20. Philip Cushman, *Constructing the Self, Constructing America* (New York: Addison-Wesley, 1995), 10, 57–61, 281.

21. David Harvey, *The Condition of Postmodernity* (Cambridge, Mass.: Basil Blackwell, 1989), 14.

22. Elizabeth M. Bounds, *Coming Together/Coming Apart: Religion, Community, and Modernity* (New York: Routledge, 1977), 32–33.

23. Ibid., 33.

24. Mary E. Hobgood, *Catholic Social Teaching and Economic Theory: Paradigms in Conflict* (Philadelphia: Temple University Press, 1991). See esp. chapter 2.

25. Susanne Kappeler, *The Will to Violence. The Politics of Personal Behavior* (New York: Columbia Teachers College Press, 1995), 29–32.

26. Judith V. Jordan, "Clarity in Connection: Empathic Knowing, Desire, and Sexuality," in *Women's Growth in Diversity*, ed. Judith V. Jordan (New York: Guilford Press, 1997), 51.

27. Harrison, "The Fate of the Middle 'Class,'" 55.

28. Contrary to those who hold, on the one hand, that we have an essential human nature or, on the other hand, that we are socially constructed in every aspect, I am persuaded by the view that who we are is what we have been able to do (some laboring under far more constraints than others) with our species nature and our concrete environmental particulars. The content of our species nature seems to be relevant in all historical and cultural contexts (e.g., basic material needs, love, friendship and respect, self-management). Our concrete environment, however, is culturally and historically specific. See Albert and Hahnel, *Unorthodox Marxism*, 118–25, 136.

29. Elizabeth Bettenhausen, "Embracing Identity: Creativity and Security" (ms, AIDS and Religion in America Convocation Papers, 1999), 4. Published on the *AIDS National Interfaith Network* Web site at www.anin.org.

30. Kristin Waters, review of *Revisioning the Political: Feminist Reconstructions of Traditional Concepts in Western Philosophy*, by Nancy J. Hirschmann and Christine Di Stefano, eds., *American Philosophical Newsletters* 96:2 (spring 1997): 39–42.

31. Joanna Macy and Molly Young Brown, *Coming Back to Life: Practices on Recovering Our Lives* (Philadelphia: New Society Publishers, 1998), 49.

32. Kappeler, *The Will to Violence*, 24–28.

33. Suzanne Pharr, *In the Time of the Right: Reflections on Liberation* (Berkeley: Chardon Press, 1996), 45.

34. Eric Mount Jr., *Professional Ethics in Context: Institutions, Images, and Empathy* (Louisville: Westminster/John Knox, 1990), 142.

35. Bettenhausen, "Embracing Identity," 3.

36. Pharr, *In the Time of the Right*, 21.

37. I am grateful to Kappeler, whose lead I am following in framing this discussion. See Kappeler, *The Will to Violence*, 20–23.

38. Pharr, *In the Time of the Right*, 1.

39. Harrison, "The Fate of the Middle 'Class.'"

40. Priscilla Pope-Levison and John R. Levison, *Jesus in Global Contexts* (Louisville: John Knox/Westminster, 1992).

41. These scholars are too numerous to list. Among the most well-known include Gustavo Gutiérrez, Jon Sobrino, Juan Louis Segundo, Leonardo Boff, Jose Miguez Bonino, Aloysius Pieris, Chung Hyun Kyung, C. S. Song, Justin S. Ukpong, Mercy Amba Oduyoye, and John S. Mbiti.

42. Marcus J. Borg, *Jesus in Contemporary Scholarship* (Valley Forge, Pa.: Trinity Press, 1994), 9. In addition to Borg, these scholars include John Dominic Crossan, Elisabeth Schüssler Fiorenza, Richard Horsley, Norman Gottwald, Bernard Lee, and Richard J. Cassidy.

43. Ibid., 101–17.

44. Ibid., 29.

45. Robert A. Ludwig, "Reconstructing Jesus for a Dysfunctional Church," in *Jesus and Faith: A Conversation on the Work of John Dominic Crossan*, ed. Jeffrey Carlson and Robert A. Ludwig (Maryknoll, N.Y.: Orbis Books, 1994), 64–67.

46. Catherine Keller, "The Jesus of History and the Feminism of Theology," in *Jesus and Faith*, 71–82.

47. Quoted in Borg, *Jesus in Contemporary Scholarship*, 25.

48. Hobgood, *Catholic Social Teaching*. See esp. chapter 6.

49. Ibid., 154–55.

50. This is true of the entire tradition of Catholic social teaching. See Hobgood, *Catholic Social Teaching*.

51. Gloria H. Albrecht, *The Character of Our Communities: Toward an Ethic of Liberation for the Church* (Nashville: Abingdon Press, 1995), 148.

52. Bounds, *Coming Together/Coming Apart*, 38.

53. Henry Giroux, *Fugitive Cultures: Race, Violence, and Youth* (New York: Routledge, 1996), 184.

54. Stanley A. Deetz, *Democracy in an Age of Corporate Colonization* (Albany: State University of New York Press, 1992), 159.

55. Donna Bivens, quoted in Marian Meck Groot, "The Heart Cannot Express Its Goodness," *The Brown Papers* 3, no. 5 (February 1997): 1.

56. Norman K. Gottwald, "Values and Economic Structures," in *Religion and Economic Justice*, ed. Michael Zweig (Philadelphia: Temple University Press, 1991), 53–77.

57. Hannah Arendt, *Eichmann in Jerusalem: A Report on the Banality of Evil* (New York: Viking, 1963).

58. Beverly Wildung Harrison, "Theological Reflection in the Struggle for Liberation," in *Making the Connections: Essays in Feminist Social Ethics*, ed. Carol Robb (Boston: Beacon Press, 1985), 260.

2. Dismantling Whiteness

1. People of color are diverse and heterogeneous groups in the United States that include African Americans, Latinos, Chicanos, American Indians, Asian Americans, and Arab Americans, among others.

2. Written communication to Mary E. Hobgood, 18 February 1999. Reprinted by permission.

3. Maria Lugones, "*Hablando cara a cara*/Speaking Face to Face: An Exploration of Ethnocentric Racism," in *Making Face, Making Soul: Creative and Critical Perspectives by Feminists of Color*, ed. Gloria Anzaldúa (San Francisco: Aunt Lute Books, 1990), 48–49.

4. McIntosh, "White Privilege and Male Privilege."

5. Harrison, "The Fate of the Middle 'Class,'" 55.

6. Ada María Isasi-Díaz, "Solidarity: Love of Neighbor in the 1980s," in *Feminist Theological Ethics*, ed. Lois K. Daly (Louisville: Westminster/John Knox, 1994), 82.

7. Bannerji, "But Who Speaks for Us?" 116.

8. Iris Marion Young, "Asymmetrical Reciprocity: On Moral Respect, Wonder, and Enlarged Thought," *Constellations* 3:3 (1997): 349.

9. Ibid., 360.

10. For example, even poorer working-class white males benefit from race-segregated and gender-segregated labor and the lower relative income received by people of color and white women.

11. Ruth Frakenberg, "When We Are Capable of Stopping, We Begin to

See: Being White, Seeing Whiteness," in *Names We Call Home: Autobiography on Racial Identity*, ed. Becky Thompson and Sangeeta Tyagi (New York: Routledge, 1996), 15.

12. Noel Ignatiev, *How the Irish Became White* (New York: Routledge, 1995), 115–16. See also Karen Brodkin, *How Jews Became White Folks and What That Says about Race in America* (New Brunswick, N.J.: Rutgers University Press, 1999).

13. David R. Roediger, *The Wages of Whiteness: Race and the Making of the American Working Class* (New York: Verso, 1991).

14. Ibid., 151–54.

15. Cushman, *Constructing the Self*, 50.

16. Ibid., 16.

17. Roediger, *The Wages of Whiteness*, 115–31; and Cushman, *Constructing the Self*, 41–52.

18. Herbert Marcuse, *One Dimensional Man* (Boston: Beacon Press, 1964), 59.

19. Ibid., 70. Contrary to another member of the Frankfurt School, Jürgen Habermas, who is discussed in the last chapter, Marcuse did not believe in the possibility of social emancipation. He held that social forces had created a "one dimensional society" in which bureaucratic control and cultural manipulation produced the "decline of the individual."

20. Cushman, *Constructing the Self*, 52.

21. Walter Brueggemann, *The Prophetic Imagination* (Minneapolis: Fortress Press, 1978), 45.

22. Herbert Marcuse, *Eros and Civilization: A Philosophical Inquiry into Freud* (Boston: Beacon Press, 1955), 203–8.

23. Cushman, *Constructing the Self*, 52; and Roediger, *The Wages of Whiteness*, 97.

24. Roediger, *The Wages of Whiteness*, 58.

25. Ibid., 12.

26. Ann Withorn, "Why My Mother Slapped Me," in *For Crying Out Loud: Women's Poverty in the United States*, ed. Ann Withorn and Diane Dujon (Boston: South End Press, 1996), 13–16.

27. bell hooks, *Killing Rage: Ending Racism* (New York: Henry Holt, 1995), 31–50.

28. Ibid., 54.

29. Marilyn Frye, "White Woman Feminist," in *Overcoming Racism and Sexism*, ed. Linda A. Bell and David Blumenfield (Lanham, Md.: Rowman & Littlefield, 1995), 119.

30. Quoted in Bounds, *Coming Together/Coming Apart*, 96.

31. Roediger, *The Wages of Whiteness*, 177.

32. Rose M. Brewer, "Theorizing Race, Class, and Gender," in *Materialist Feminism: A Reader in Class, Difference, and Women's Lives*, ed. Rosemary Hennessy and Chrys Ingraham (New York: Routledge, 1997), 239.

33. Paul Kivel, *Uprooting Racism* (Philadelphia: New Society Publishers, 1996), 79.

34. Robert John Ackerman, *Heterogeneities: Race, Gender, Class, Nation, and State* (Amherst: University of Massachusetts Press, 1996), 1–7.

35. McIntosh, "White Privilege and Male Privilege."

36. Ibid., 5–9.

37. Manning Marable, *How Capitalism Underdeveloped Black America: Problems in Race, Political Economy, and Society* (Boston: South End Press, 1983).

38. Kivel, *Uprooting Racism*, 133, 143.

39. Marc Cooper, "The Heartland's Raw Deal: How Meatpacking Is Creating a New Immigrant Underclass," *The Nation*, 3 February 1997, 11–17.

40. Kivel, *Uprooting Racism*, 29–30.

41. Ackerman, *Heterogeneities*, 36.

42. Arthur Brittan and Mary Meynard, *Sexism, Racism, and Oppression* (New York: Basil Blackwell, 1984), 50.

43. bell hooks, *Black Looks: Race and Representation* (Boston: South End Press, 1992), 21–39.

44. Ibid., 39.

45. Kivel, *Uprooting Racism*, 137–38.

46. Ibid., 167.

47. About 39 percent of AFDC families have been white; 37 percent black; 18 percent Latino; 3 percent Asian; and 1 percent American Indian. See Holly Sklar, *Chaos or Community: Seeking Solutions, Not Scapegoats for Bad Economics* (Boston: South End Press, 1995), 94.

48. Ibid., 126.

49. Young, "Asymmetrical Reciprocity," 345.

50. Ann Ferguson, *Sexual Democracy: Women, Oppression, and Revolution* (San Francisco: Westview Press, 1995), 115.

51. Stephanie M. Wildman, *Privilege Revealed: How Invisible Preference Undermines America* (New York: New York University Press, 1996), 85–102.

52. bell hooks, *Killing Rage*, 224.

53. Sharon D. Welch, *Sweet Dreams in America: Making Ethics and Spirituality Work* (New York: Routledge, 1999), 131.

54. Kate McKenna, "Subjects of Discourse: Learning the Language That Counts," in *Unsettling Relations: The University as a Site of Feminist Struggle* (Boston: South End Press, 1996), 121.

55. Joni Seager, "Creating a Culture of Destruction: Gender, Militarism, and the Environment," in *Toxic Struggles: The Theory and Practice of Environmental Justice*, ed. Richard Hofrichter (Philadelphia: New Society Publishers, 1993), 63.

56. Robert D. Bullard, "Anatomy of Environmental Racism," in *Toxic Struggles*, 30.

57. Seager, "Creating a Culture of Destruction," 63.

58. Ibid.

59. Cynthia Hamilton, "Environmental Consequences of Urban Growth and Blight," in *Toxic Struggles*, 71.

60. Daniel Faber and James O'Connor, "Capitalism and Crisis of Environmentalism," in *Toxic Struggles*, 14.

61. Larry L. Rasmussen, *Earth Community, Earth Ethics* (Maryknoll, N.Y.: Orbis Books, 1996), 75–110.

62. Kivel, *Uprooting Racism*, 36–37, 50.

63. Toni Morrison, quoted in Kappeler, *The Will to Violence*, 54.

64. Albrecht, *The Character of Our Communities*, 164.

65. Kivel, *Uprooting Racism*, 36–37.

66. Barbara Smith, "Between a Rock and A Hard Place," in *Yours in the Struggle: Three Feminist Perspectives on Anti-Semitism and Racism*, ed. Elly Bulkin, Minnie Bruce Pratt, and Barbara Smith (Ithaca, N.Y.: Firebrand Books, 1984), 74.

67. Quoted in Becky Thompson, "Time Traveling and Border Crossing: Reflections on White Identity," in *Names We Call Home*, 103.

68. Bryan N. Massingale, "The Ethics of Racism," *Origins* 28 (26 November 1998), 425–26.

69. National Conference of Catholic Bishops, *Brothers and Sisters to Us: U.S. Bishops' Pastoral Letter on Racism in Our Day* (Washington, D.C.: U.S. Catholic Conference, 1979).

70. Massingale, "The Ethics of Racism," 424–28.

71. National Conference of Catholic Bishops, *Brothers and Sisters to Us*, 6.

72. Ibid., 3.

73. Ibid., 10–13.

74. See also Black Bishops of the United States, "What We Have Seen and Heard: Pastoral Letter of Evangelization," *Origins* 14 (18 October 1984): 282; National Conference of Catholic Bishops, *Heritage and Hope: Evangelization in the United States* (Washington, D.C.: U.S. Catholic Conference, 1991), 2; and Massingale, "The Ethics of Racism," n. 18.

75. Cynthia Garcia Coll, Robin Cook-Nobles, and Janet L. Surrey, "Building Connection through Diversity," in *Women's Growth in Diversity*, 187.

76. Ferguson, *Sexual Democracy*, 127.

77. Kappeler, *The Will to Violence*, 234.

78. bell hooks, *Killing Rage*, 263–65; and Gloria Yamato, "Something about the Subject Makes It Hard to Name," in *Making Face, Making Soul*, 24.

79. John Anner, ed., *Beyond Identity Politics: Emerging Social Justice Movements in Communities of Color* (Boston: South End Press, 1996).

80. Becky Thompson and Sangeeta Tyagi, "Story Telling as Social Conscience," in *Names We Call Home*, xv.

81. Kivel, *Uprooting Racism*, 205.

82. Bounds, *Coming Together/Coming Apart*, 21.

83. Ibid., 89.

84. Ibid., 120.

85. W. E. B. DuBois, *The Gift of Black Folk*, quoted in Roediger, *The Wages of Whiteness*, 180.

86. Sharon D. Welch, "Dreams of the Common Good: From the Analytics of Oppression to the Politics of Transformation," in *New Visions for the Americas: Religious Engagement and Social Transformation*, ed. David Batstone (Minneapolis: Fortress Press, 1993), 187.

87. Melanie Kaye/Kantrowitz, "Jews in the U.S.: The Rising Costs of Whiteness," in *Names We Call Home*, 134.

3. An Economic Ethics of Right Relationship

1. Greider, *One World Ready or Not: The Manic Logic of Global Capitalism* (New York: Simon & Schuster, 1997), 337–38.

2. Harvey, *Justice*, 334–38.

3. John O'Connor, "The Promise of Environmental Democracy," in *Toxic Struggles*, 47.

4. Norman K. Gottwald, "Values and Economic Structures," in *Religion and Economic Justice*, Michael Zweig, ed. (Philadelphia: Temple University Press, 1991), 55.

5. Michael Lerner, "Jewish Liberation Theology," in *Religion and Economic Justice*, 131–33.

6. Gottwald, "Values and Economic Structures," 55–56.

7. Ibid., 57.

8. Borg, *Jesus in Contemporary Scholarship*, 104, 117.

9. Gottwald, "Values and Economic Structures," 58.

10. Carol S. Robb, *Equal Value: An Ethical Approach to Economics and Sex* (Boston: Beacon Press, 1995), 142–45.

11. See Hobgood, *Catholic Social Teaching*, esp. 228–37.

12. *Sollicitudo Rei Socialis* (1987), 42. The official English texts of Catholic documents can be found in David J. O'Brien and Thomas A. Shannon, eds., *Catholic Social Teaching: The Documentary Heritage* (Maryknoll, N.Y.: Orbis Books, 1992). I follow the standard convention of using Latin names for documents originating in Rome and standard paragraph or section numbers for all documents.

13. *Centesimus Annus* (1991), 40.

14. *Laborem Exercens* (1981), 12, 14.

15. *Ethical Choices and Political Challenges* (1983), 13.

16. Ibid., 6.

17. Puebla (1979), 96, 733, 1134, 1136, 1142, 1145, 1217.

18. Hobgood, *Catholic Social Teaching*, 159–60.

19. Gottwald, "Values and Economic Structures," 67.

20. Max Weber, *The Theory of Social and Economic Organization*, ed. Talcott Parsons (New York: Free Press, 1964), 424–29.

21. Lawrence Mishal, Jared Bernstein, and John Schmitt, *The State of Working America, 1998–99* (Ithaca, N.Y.: Cornell University Press, 1999), 51.

22. For Marx's discussions on class, which are scattered throughout his work, see David McLellan, *Karl Marx: Selected Writings* (New York: Oxford University Press, 1977). See subsequent elaborations by Marxist theoreticians such as Maurice Dobb, *Studies in the Development of Capitalism* (New York: International Publishers, 1964); Harry Braverman, *Labor and Monopoly Capital* (New York: Monthly Review Press, 1974); and Albert and Hahnel, *Unorthodox Marxism.*

23. Ferguson, *Sexual Democracy*, 35. Ferguson says that the notion of work here involves not only the production of things and services but also the production of people. However, we separate the two since they have different "logics" and feminist and class theoreticians still have work to do to better elucidate how the production of things and services and the production of people are deeply intertwined. Ibid., 69.

24. Mishel et al., *The State of Working America*, 256–58, and Council on International and Public Affairs, "Why Today's Big Profits Mean Big Trouble," *Too Much*, fall 1995, 1.

25. Ibid., 258–60.

26. Manning Marable, *Black Liberation in Conservative America* (Boston: South End Press, 1997), 24.

27. See Barbara and John Ehrenreich, "The Professional-Managerial Class," in *Between Labor and Capital*, ed. Pat Walker (Montreal: Black Rose Books, 1978), 5–45. While the Ehrenreichs see this group as a separate class whose role is to produce capitalist ideology and control the working class, I prefer to emphasize the common class position that professionals and managers share with laborers vis-à-vis capital.

28. Mishel et al., *The State of Working America*, 134. It is important to be clear, however, that capitalism means something different for women than for men because capitalist relations of production are built upon patriarchal relations of reproduction. Women who work harder for less in the public workforce also work for nothing in the home, bearing the burden of a double working day. How capitalism and patriarchy are intertwined will be addressed in chapter 4.

29. The Michael Harrington Center for Democratic Values and Social Action, Queens College, CUNY, "An Update on the Economic Status of Women," *Action Brief* 4 (1998).

30. Marable, *Black Liberation*, 262.

31. See *Money, Income of Households, Families, and Persons in the U.S. 1992* (CPR, P-60), B-37; and Census Bureau, *Income, Poverty, and Valuation of Noncash Benefits*, 1993, prepublication press excerpts (October 1994).

32. Chuck Collins, Betsy Leondar-Wright, and Holly Sklar, *Shifting Fortunes: Thje Perils of the Growing American Wealth Gap* (Boston: United for a Fair Economy, 1999), 55–57.

33. Michael Zweig, "Class and Poverty in the U.S. Economy," in *Religion and Economic Justice*, 211.

34. Mishel et al., *The State of Working America*, 130.

35. See, for example, Joan Greenbaum, *Windows on the Workplace: Computers, Jobs, and the Organization of Office Work in the Late Twentieth Century* (New York: Monthly Review Press, 1995); and Barbara Hilkert Andolsen, *The New Job Contract: Economic Justice in an Age of Insecurity* (Cleveland: The Pilgrim Press, 1998).

36. Juliet B. Shor, *The Overworked American* (New York: Basic Books, 1991).

37. Greenbaum, *Windows on the Workplace*, 19–21, 93.

38. Carmen Vasquez, "Walking on Moonsands," in *Racism in the Lives of Women*, ed. Jeanne Adleman and Gloria Enguidanos (Binghamton, N.Y.: Harrington Park Press, 1995), 7.

39. Greenbaum, *Windows on the Workplace*; Andolsen, *The New Job Contract*; and William K. Tabb, "Globalization Is *An* Issue, the Power of Capital Is *The* Issue," *Monthly Review* 49:2 (June 1997): 29 n. 3.

40. Mishel et al., *The State of Working America*, 51.

41. Zweig, "Class and Poverty," 208; see also Kim Moody, *Workers in a Lean World: Unions in the International Economy* (London: Verso, 1997), 188.

42. Mishel et al., *The State of Working America*, 51.

43. Diana Pierce and Laura Russell, *The Self-Sufficiency Standard for Massachusetts* (Wider Opportunities for Women: Women's Educational and Industrial Union, Sept. 1998), 7–9, 46.

44. Mishel et al., *The State of Working America*, 137.

45. Tabb, "Globalization Is *An* Issue," 27.

46. Shor, *The Overworked American*, 22, 150.

47. Mishel et al., *The State of Working America*, 131.

48. Ibid., 173.

49. Greenbaum, *Windows on the Workplace*, 18, 26, 31, 45, 48.

50. Ibid., 96.

51. Shor, *The Overworked American*, 39.

52. Kebebew Ashagrie, "Statistics on Working Children and Hazardous Child Labour," *International Labour* Office: Geneva, Switzerland, 1997–98, International Labor Organization (ILO) @http://www.ilo.org/public/english/child/documentation/trends/stats.htm.

53. Greider, *One World Ready or Not*, 341, 348; and Douglas Kruse and Douglas Mahoney, "Illegal Child Labor in the United States: Prevalence and Characteristics," *National Bureau of Economic Research, Inc.*, 1998, working paper number 6479@http://www.nber.org/papers/w6479.

54. Kenneth M. Dolbeare, *Democracy at Risk: The Politics of Economic Renewal* (Chatham, N.J.: Chatham House Publishers, 1986), 217.

55. Salim Muwakkil, "My Own Private Alcatraz," *In These Times* 21, no. 3 (23 December 1996): 24–25.

56. Marable, *Black Liberation*, 48; and Leon Friedman, "A Share the Wealth Tax," *The Nation*, 6 January 1997, 23-24.

57. Harvey, *Justice*, 348.

58. Ibid., 347.

59. Kappeler, *The Will to Violence*, 216.

60. Elizabeth V. Spellman, *Fruits of Sorrow: Framing Our Attention to Suffering* (Boston: Beacon Press, 1997).

61. Albrecht, *The Character of Our Communities*, 162.

62. Harrison, "Theological Reflection," 246.

63. Greider, *One World Ready or Not*, 336, 359.

64. Ibid., 45-48.

65. Ibid., 48.

66. David Loy, "The Religion of the Market," *Journal of the American Academy of Religion* 65, no. 2 (summer 1997): 283.

67. Harvey, *Justice*, 339.

68. Tom Roberts, "New Battles Brew over Defense Spending, Arms Sales," *National Catholic Reporter* 35, no. 36 (13 August 1999): 14.

69. Sklar, *Chaos or Community*, 149.

70. Ramsey Clark, Sean Gervasi, Sara Flounders, Nadja Tesich, Thomas Deichmann and others, *NATO in the Balkans: Voices of Opposition* (New York: International Action Center, 1998).

71. Quoted in Sklar, *Chaos or Community*, 35.

72. Greg Albo, "The World Economy, Market Imperatives, and Alternatives," *Monthly Review* 48:7 (December 1996): 7.

73. Greider, *One World Ready or Not*, 48.

74. Tabb, "Globalization Is *An* Issue," 22.

75. Piven and Cloward, "Eras of Power," 20.

76. George Ritzer, *The McDonaldization of Society* (Thousand Oaks, Calif.: Pine Forge Press, 1996), 79-99.

77. Harvey, *The Condition of Postmodernity*, 107.

78. Ibid., 147, 153, 174.

79. Ibid., 159.

80. Ynestra King, "Feminism and Ecology," in *Toxic Struggles*, 77.

81. Harvey, *The Condition of Postmodernity*, 229.

82. Deetz, *Democracy in an Age of Corporate Colonization*, 226, 294.

83. Harvey, *The Condition of Postmodernity*, 287

84. Greenbaum, *Windows on the Workplace*, 77.

85. Loy, "The Religion of the Market," 287.

86. Deetz, *Democracy in an Age of Corporate Colonization*, 209.

87. Ibid., 215.

88. Ibid., 210.

89. Beverly Harrison, "The Ideological Spectrum: How Values Are Transformed in the Real World," *Advocating Justice and Equality: A Policy Resource Guide* (Elkhart, Ind.: National Council of the Churches of Christ USA, 1998), 21.

90. Marc Estrin, "If Not Mean-Spirited, What Are They?" *Peacework* 254 (July–August 1995): 10.

91. Margaret Cerullo and Marla Erlien, "Beyond the Normal Family," in *For Crying Out Loud: Women and Poverty in the United States*, ed. Rachel Lefkowitz and Ann Withorn (New York: The Pilgrim Press, 1988), 252.

92. Carole Pateman, *The Sexual Contract* (Cambridge: Polity Press, 1988), 149.

93. Estrin, "If Not Mean-Spirited," 10.

94. United Nations Development Programme (UNDP), *Human Development Report 1992* (New York: Oxford University Press, 1992); and Daniel C. McGuire and Larry L. Rasmussen, *Ethics for a Small Planet: New Horizons on Population, Consumption, and Ecology* (Albany: State University of New York Press, 1998), 8, 18.

95. UNDP, *Human Development Report 1992*; and UNDP, *Human Development Report 1997* (New York: Oxford University Press, 1997).

96. Greider, *One World Ready or Not*, 390, 404–6.

97. Edward S. Herman, *Triumph of the Market* (Boston: South End Press, 1995), 5.

98. For more information contact the AFL-CIO at 408-761-7173.

99. Cooper, "The Heartland's Raw Deal," 11–17.

100. Harvey, *The Condition of Postmodernity*, 303.

101. Peter J. Haas, *Morality After Auschwitz: The Radical Challenge of the Nazi Ethic* (Philadelphia: Fortress Press, 1988), 170.

102. Paul Farmer, Margaret Connors, and Janie Simmons, eds., *Women, Poverty, and AIDS* (Monroe, Maine: Common Courage Press, 1996).

103. Stan Grossfeld, "New Dangers Make Way to US Tables," *Boston Sunday Globe*, 20 September 1998, sec. A.

104. Minnie Bruce Pratt, *Rebellion: Essays 1980–1991* (Ithaca, N.Y.: Firebrand Books, 1991), 118–21.

105. Ibid., 121.

106. Deetz, *Democracy in an Age of Corporate Colonization*, 203.

107. Greider, *One World Ready or Not*, 216.

108. Sklar, *Chaos or Community*, 44–46; Greider, *One World Ready or Not*, 64–65; and Greenbaum, *Windows on the Workplace*, 120, 129.

109. Greenbaum, *Windows on the Workplace*, 124.

110. Greider, *One World Ready or Not*, 73; and Sklar, *Chaos or Community*, 26.

111. Greenbaum, *Windows on the Workplace*, 130.

112. Herman, *Triumph of the Market*, 14.

113. Greenbaum, *Windows on the Workplace*; and Andolsen, *The New Job Contract*.

114. Greider, *One World Ready or Not*, 43.

115. Ibid., 43.

116. Greenbaum, *Windows on the Workplace*, 133.

117. Robert J. Samuelson, "Why We're Married to the Market," *Newsweek*, 27 April 1998, 50.

118. John Leland, "Blessed Be the Bull," *Newsweek*, 27 April 1998, 52.

119. Michael Meyer, "Tales from the Sardine Run," *Newsweek*, 27 April 1998, 58, 60.

120. Katha Pollitt, "Let Them Eat Numbers," *The Nation*, 30 December 1996, 8.

121. Harrison, "Theological Reflection," 247.

122. Christine E. Gudorf, *Body, Sex, and Pleasure: Reconstructing Christian Sexual Ethics* (Cleveland: The Pilgrim Press, 1994), 160–204.

123. Robert N. Bellah, "Class Wars and Culture Wars in the University Today," *Council of Societies for the Study of Religion Bulletin* 27, no. 1 (February 1998): 2.

124. Quoted in bell hooks, *Outlaw Culture: Resisting Representations* (New York: Routledge, 1995), 246.

125. Margaret Talbot, "Attachment Theory: The Ultimate Experiment," *New York Times Magazine*, 24 May 1998, 24–54.

126. Lawrence Mordekhai Thomas, "Power, Trust, and Evil," in *Overcoming Racism and Sexism*, ed. Linda A. Bell and David Blumenfeld (Lanham, Md.: Rowman & Littlefield, 1995), 160.

127. Ibid., 158–61.

128. Loy, "The Religion of the Market," 288.

129. Harrison, "Theological Reflection," 243.

130. Kenneth Westhuis, "Reginald Bibby's Preference for the Market Model in the Sociology of Religion," *The Ecumenist* 3, no. 1 (January–March 1996): 7.

131. Adam Phillips, "Satisfaction Not Guaranteed," *New York Times Magazine*, 7 June 1998, 82.

132. "Measures of Pleasure," *Women's Review of Books* 15, nos. 10–11 (July 1988): 11, 13.

133. Alice Walker, *Anything We Love Can Be Saved* (New York: Ballantine Books, 1997), 55, 196.

134. To identify the potential for working-class solidarity in the highly segmented intermediate sector, see Carolyn Howe, *Political Ideology and Class Formation: A Study of the Middle Class* (Westport, Conn.: Praeger, 1992), esp. chapters 5 and 7.

135. Ibid., 152.

136. Ferguson, *Sexual Democracy*, 175–76.

137. Bleifuss, "Warfare or Welfare," *In These Times* 21, no. 2 (9 December 1996): 14.

138. Puebla (1979), 525; see also 806, 1046, 1054.

4. Constructing a Compassionate Sexuality

1. Gail Rubin, "The Traffic in Women: Notes on the 'Political Economy' of Sex," in *Toward an Anthropology of Women*, ed. Rayna Reiter (New York: Monthly Review Press, 1975).

2. Chrys Ingraham, "The Heterosexual Imaginary: Feminist Sociology and Theories of Gender," in *Materialist Feminism*, 286–87.

3. Some of this expanding work includes Paula Gun Allen, ed., *Spider Woman's Granddaughters: Traditional Tales and Contemporary Writing by Native American Women* (New York: Fawcett Columbine, 1989); Cherrie Moraga and Gloria Anzaldúa, eds., *This Bridge Called My Back: Writings by Radical Women of Color* (New York: Kitchen Table Press, 1981); Gloria T. Hull, Patricia Bell Scott, and Barbara Smith, eds., *All the Women Are White, All the Blacks Are Men, But Some of Us Are Brave* (New York: Feminist Press, 1982); bell hooks, *Feminist Theory: From Margin to Center* (Boston: South End Press, 1984); Barbara Christian, *Black Feminist Criticism* (New York: Pergamon Press, 1985); Anzaldúa, *Making Face, Making Soul*; Patricia Hill Collins, *Black Feminist Thought: Knowledge, Consciousness, and the Politics of Empowerment* (New York: Routledge & Kegan Paul, 1991); Elaine H. Kim, Lilia A. Villanueva, and Asian Women United of California, eds., *Making More Waves: New Writing by Asian American Women* (Boston: Beacon Press, 1997); Carla Trujillo, ed., *Living Chicana Theory* (Berkeley: Third Women Press, 1998).

4. Ferguson, *Sexual Democracy*, 114–15.

5. Brewer, "Theorizing Race, Class, and Gender," 246.

6. Carby, "White Women Listen!" 115.

7. Brittan and Maynard, *Sexism, Racism, and Oppression*, 56.

8. The Michael Harrington Center for Democratic Values and Social Action, "An Update on the Economic Status of Women."

9. As compared to 11.6 percent of white men, 19.4 percent of black men, and 26.4 percent of Latinos who also made less than $13,091 in 1992. Sklar, *Chaos or Community*, 22.

10. As compared to 16.4 percent of white men, 5.1 percent of black men, and 5.3 percent of Latinos who earned above $52,364 for full-time work in 1992. Ibid.

11. Mishel et al., *The State of Working America*, 172.

12. Brewer, "Theorizing Race, Class, and Gender," 244.

13. Nancy Fraser, *Justice Interruptus: Critical Reflections on the "Postsocialist" Condition* (New York: Routledge, 1997), 228.

14. Cynthia R. Comacchio, "Motherhood in Crisis," in *Materialist Feminism*, 306–27.

15. John D'Emilio, "Capitalism and Gay Identity," in *The Lesbian and Gay Studies Reader*, ed. Henry Ablelove, Michele Aina Barale, and David M. Halperin (New York: Routledge, 1993), 467–78.

16. Ingraham, "The Heterosexual Imaginary," 283; and U.S. Dept. of Labor, Women's Bureau, *1993 Handbook on Women Workers: Trends and Issues* (Washington, D.C., 1993), 232–33. Quoted in Gloria H. Albrecht, "The Production of Character," *Welfare Policy: Feminist Critiques*, ed. Elizabeth M. Bounds, Pamela K. Brubaker, and Mary E. Hobgood (Cleveland: The Pilgrim Press, 1999), 103.

17. Maguire and Rasmussen, *Ethics for a Small Planet*, 3.

18. Meera Nanda, "History Is What Hurts: A Materialist Feminist Perspective on the Green Revolution and its Ecofeminist Critics," in *Materialist Feminism*, 373–81.

19. Carby, "White Women Listen!" 110–28.

20. Ferguson, *Sexual Democracy*, 40, 115.

21. Harrison, "Theological Reflection," 3–21.

22. Marvin M. Ellison, *Erotic Justice: A Liberating Ethic of Sexuality* (Louisville: Westminster John Knox, 1996), 8.

23. Ibid., 45.

24. Gudorf, *Body, Sex, and Pleasure*, 176.

25. Lori L. Heise, "Violence, Sexuality, and Women's Lives," in *The Gender Sexuality Reader: Culture, History, and Political Economy*, ed. Roger N. Lancaster and Michaela di Leonardo (New York: Routledge, 1997), 414.

26. Ibid., 414.

27. Marcuse, *Eros and Civilization*, 199–222.

28. Comacchio, "Motherhood in Crisis," 311.

29. Linda Singer, *Erotic Welfare: Sexual Theory and Politics in the Age of Epidemic* (New York: Routledge, 1993), 39.

30. Kivel, *Uprooting Racism*, 66.

31. Evelyn Brooks Higginbotham, "African-American Women's History and the Metalanguage of Race," *Signs: Journal of Women in Culture and Society* 17:2 (1992): 254.

32. Collins, *Black Feminist Thought*, 174.

33. Patricia J. Williams, "Mr. Lincoln's Legacy," *The Nation*, 26 October 1998, 9.

34. Mary D. Pellauer, "The Moral Significance of the Female Orgasm," in *Sexuality and the Sacred: Sources for Theological Reflection*, ed. James B. Nelson and Sandra P. Longfellow (Louisville: Westminster/John Knox, 1994), 154.

35. Mary E. Hobgood, "Marriage, Market Values, and Social Justice: Toward an Examination of Compulsory Monogamy," in *Redefining Sexual Ethics*, ed. Eleanor H. Haney and Susan E. Davies (Cleveland: The Pilgrim Press, 1991), 115–26.

36. Gudorf, *Body, Sex, and Pleasure*, 160–204.

37. Alice Miller, *The Drama of the Gifted Child* (New York: Basic Books, 1994) and *For Your Own Good: Hidden Cruelty in Child-Rearing and the Roots of Violence* (New York: Farrar, Straus & Giroux, 1983), 231.

38. Ellison, *Erotic Justice*, 50.

39. Lise Vogel, "From the Women's Question to Women's Liberation," in *Materialist Feminism*, 144.

40. Leslie Feinburg, "Transgender Liberation," in *Materialist Feminism*, 230.

41. Ingraham, "The Heterosexual Imaginary," 287.

42. Feinburg, "Transgender Liberation," 229.

43. Ibid., 229–30.

44. Maria Mies, "Colonization and Housewifizaton," in *Materialist Feminism*, 177.

45. Heise, "Violence, Sexuality, and Women's Lives," 424–25.

46. Peggy Reeves Sanday, "The Socio-Cultural Context of Rape: A Cross-Cultural Study," *Journal of Social Issues* 37, no. 4 (1981): 5–27.

47. Heise, "Violence, Sexuality, and Women's Lives," 424.

48. James B. Nelson, *The Intimate Connection: Male Sexuality, Masculinist Spirituality* (Philadelphia: Westminster Press, 1988), 80.

49. Classical literature on the origins of the heteronormative monogamous family includes the following: Johann Bachofen, *Das Mutterrecht* (Berlin: Bauhaus-Archiv, 1861); Lewis Henry Morgan, *Ancient Society* (Cambridge, Mass.: Belknap Press, 1877); Frederick Engels, *The Origins of the Family, Private Property, and the State* (New York: International, 1884); Eli Zaretsky, *Capitalism, the Family, and Personal Life* (New York: Harper & Row, 1976).

50. Feinberg, "Transgender Liberation," 231.

51. Ingraham, "The Heterosexual Imaginary," 289.

52. Carby, "White Women Listen!" 123.

53. Howard Zinn, *A People's History of the United States* (New York: Harper & Row, 197), 21.

54. Paul Kivel, *Men's Work: How to Stop the Violence That Tears Our Lives Apart* (New York: Ballantine Books, 1992), 2.

55. Arlie Russell Hochschild, "There's No Place Like Work," *New York Times Magazine*, 20 April 1997, 51–84.

56. Arlie Hochschild and Anne Machung, "Men Who Share the Second Shift," in *Windows on Society*, 4th ed., ed. John W. Heeren and Marylee Mason (Los Angeles: Roxbury Publishing, 1996), 158–68. This is true across class lines. Hochschild and Machung also found that if a husband made *less* than his wife or had no job, he did *no* domestic labor, making up in patriarchal privilege what he lost over his wife in class privilege.

57. Ibid., 158, 166.

58. Ibid., 166.

59. Hochschild, "There's No Place Like Work," 84.

60. Ruth Sidel, *Women and Children Last: The Plight of Poor Women in Affluent America* (New York: Penguin Books, 1986), 17.

61. Beverly Wildung Harrison, "Sexuality and Social Policy," in *Sexuality and the Sacred*, 244.

62. Macy and Brown, *Coming Back to Life*, 34–35.

63. Harrison, "Sexuality and Social Policy," 243.

64. Ellison, *Erotic Justice*, 91.

65. Ibid., 37.

66. Nicola Field, "Identity and the Lifestyle Market," in *Materialist Feminism*, 264.

67. Harrison, "Theological Reflection," 225.

68. Samuel Laeuchli, *Power and Sexuality: The Emergence of Canon Law at the Synod of Elvira* (Philadelphia: Temple University Press, 1972), 88.

69. Ellison, *Erotic Justice*, 61.

70. Pius XI, "On Christian Marriage," in *Seven Great Encyclicals*, ed. William J. Gibbons, S.J. (New York/Paramus, N.J.: Paulist Press, 1963), 77–117.

71. Beverly Wildung Harrison and Carter Heyward, "Pain and Pleasure: Avoiding the Confusions of Christian Tradition in Feminist Theory," in *Sexuality and the Sacred*, 131–40.

72. Margaret A. Farley, "An Ethic for Same-Sex Relations," in *A Challenge to Love: Gay and Lesbian Relations in the Church*, ed. Robert Nugent (New York: Crossroad, 1986), 93.

73. Barbara Hilkert Andolsen, "Whose Sexuality? Whose Tradition? Women, Experience, and Roman Catholic Sexual Ethics," in *Feminist Ethics and the Catholic Moral Tradition*, ed. Charles E. Curran, Margaret A. Farley, and Richard A. McCormick, S.J. (New York/Mahwah, N.J.: Paulist Press, 1996), 207, 210.

74. Gudorf, *Body, Sex, and Pleasure*, 2.

75. Mary E. Hunt, "Sexual Ethics: A Lesbian Perspective," *Open Hands* 4, no. 3 (winter 1989): 10.

76. Macy and Brown, *Coming Back to Life*, 52–59.

77. Sandra Lipsitz Bem, *An Unconventional Family* (New Haven, Conn.: Yale University Press, 1998), 123. People are developing a larger sexual repertoire. But as in the case of Bill Clinton, they are refusing to call it sex. Ironically, in a sexually restrictive culture, this looks like an attempt to "out-orthodox the orthodox" as people claim some semblance of freedom outside male-focused genital sex that, because of oppression, is the only sexual expression with normative status.

78. Pellauer, "The Moral Significance of the Female Orgasm," 161.

5. Relational Labor and the Politics of Solidarity

1. Janet R. Jakobsen, *Working Alliances and the Politics of Difference* (Bloomington: Indiana University Press, 1998), 128–31, 144, 153, 169–70.

2. Ibid., 7, 19, 118–19.

3. Field, "Identity and the Lifestyle Market," 264.

4. Faber and O'Connor, "Capitalism and the Crisis of Environmentalism," 22.

5. Field, "Identity and the Lifestyle Market," 264.

6. Jakobsen, *Working Alliances*, 118–19.

7. Ibid., 16, 22.

8. Ibid., 14–15.

9. Ibid., 21, 33, 146–47.

10. See Rosemary Hennessy and Rajeswari Mohan, "The Construction of Women in Three Popular Texts of Empire," 187; Field, "Identity and the Lifestyle Market," 267–69; and Carole A. Stabile, "Feminism and the Ends of Postmodernism," in *Materialist Feminism*, 395–408; and Harvey, *The Condition of Postmodernity*.

11. Pharr, *In the Time of the Right*, 79, 81.

12. Jakobsen, *Working Alliances*, 150–72.

13. Ibid., 83, 102–4.

14. See Jürgen Habermas, *The Structural Transformation of the Public Sphere: An Inquiry into a Category of Bourgeois Society*, trans. Thomas Burger and Frederick Lawrence (Cambridge: MIT Press, 1989); and Jürgen Habermas, *The Theory of Communicative Action*, vol. 2, *Lifeworld and System: A Critique of Functional Reason*, trans. Thomas McCarthy (Boston: Beacon Press, 1987).

15. Gramsci, *Selections from the Prison Notebooks*; and Carl Boggs, *The Two Revolutions: Antonio Gramsci and the Dilemmas of Western Marxism* (Boston: South End Press, 1984), 243–74.

16. For a critical evaluation of Habermas that contrasts him with Gramsci, see Fraser, *Justice Interruptus*, 69–98.

17. Stabile, "Feminism and the Ends of Postmodernism," 407.

18. Jakobsen, *Working Alliances*, 27.

19. Moody, *Workers in a Lean World*, 304–7.

20. Brueggemann, *The Prophetic Imagination*, 50.

21. See Matthew 5:4 and Luke 19:41. Brueggemann, *The Prophetic Imagination*, 60.

22. Brueggemann, *The Prophetic Imagination*, 67.

23. Bob Hebert, "House of Arrogance," *New York Times*, 20 December 1998, WK 13.

24. David M. Schribman, "One Nation Under God: How the Religious Right Changed the American Conversation," *Boston Globe Magazine*, 10 January 1999, 27–31.

25. Alan Ehrenhalt, "You Call This Progress?" review of *The Corrosion of Character* by Richard Sennett (New York: W. W. Norton, 1998), *New York Times Book Review*, 20 December 1998, 16.

26. See, for example, Anner, *Beyond Identity Politics*; Ray M. Tillman and Michael S. Cummings, eds., *The Transformations of U.S. Unions: Voices, Visions, and Strategies from the Grassroots* (Boulder, Colo.: Lynne Rienner Publishers, forthcoming); Kevin Danaher, ed., *50 Years Is Enough: The Case against the World Bank* (Boston: South End Press, 1994); Jeremy Brecher, John Brown Childs, and Jull Cutler, eds., *Global Visions: Beyond the New World Order* (Boston: South End Press, 1993); Biorn Maybury-Lewis, *The Politics of the Possible: The Brazilian Workers' Trade Union Movement* (Philadelphia: Temple Univer-

sity Press, 1994); Gail Omvedt, *We Will Smash This Prison* (London: Zed, 1980).

27. Brueggemann, *The Prophetic Imagination*, 68.

28. Ibid., 81.

29. Ibid., 81–83.

30. Ibid., 86.

31. Ibid., 88.

32. Isasi-Díaz, "Solidarity," 77–87.

33. Welch, *Sweet Dreams in America*, 21, 26.

34. Ibid., 130.

35. Rev. Roy Bourgeois, M.M., "School of the Americas: A Question of Conscience," Bernard J. Flanagan Lecture on Religion and Public Affairs, College of the Holy Cross, Worcester, Mass., 26 January 1999.

36. Collins, *Fighting Words*, 189, 240.

37. Giroux, *Fugitive Cultures*, 153–55.

38. Delores S. Williams, "Straight Talk, Plain Talk: Womanist Words about Salvation in a Social Context," in *Embracing the Spirit: Womanist Perspectives on Hope, Salvation, and Transformation*, ed. Emilie M. Townes (Maryknoll, N.Y.: Orbis Books, 1997), 119–20.

39. Moody, *Workers in a Lean World*, 310.

Index